The Great God Mogadon and Other Plays

Barry Oakley

University of Queensland Press

Published by University of Queensland Press, St Lucia,
Queensland 1980

Typeset by Press Etching Pty Ltd, Brisbane
Printed and bound by Southwood Press Pty Ltd, Sydney

Distributed in the United Kingdom, Europe, the Middle East,
Africa, and the Caribbean by Prentice-Hall International,
International Book Distributors Ltd, 66 Wood Lane End, Hemel
Hempstead, Herts., England

Published with the assistance of the Literature Board of the
Australia Council

National Library of Australia
Cataloguing-in-Publication data
Oakley, Barry, 1931-
   The great god Mogadon and other plays.

   (Contemporary Australian plays; 8 ISSN 0589-7468)
   ISBN 0 7022 1436 1
   ISBN 0 7022 1437 x Paperback

   I. Title. (Series)

A822'.3

Also by Barry Oakley

Novels

A Wild Ass of a Man
A Salute to the Great McCarthy
Let's Hear It For Prendergast

Plays

The Feet of Daniel Mannix
Beware of Imitations
Bedfellows
A Lesson In English
The Ship's Whistle
Marsupials

Short Stories

Walking Through Tigerland

For Children

How They Caught Kevin Farrelly

Contents

Introduction

Oakley seems to have been around longer than any of us. Wry, sceptical, his nervy drolleries and implacable sense of irony have helped him survive over twelve years in an increasingly neurotic, paranoid and self-destructive local theatre.

He has endured dozens of violent meetings at the Pram Factory, terrible rehearsals, poor performances of his plays, terrible arguments about the morality of his work and more kitchen politics than Len Evans.

One can only assume that his background in the Public Service has enabled him to cope with the meetings and his education with the Christian Brothers has given him a Friend to help him through the rest.

One lesson he seems to have learned very early on is that the best preparation for a life in the theatre is not Stanislavski, but the collected memoirs of Kim Philby, and certainly his tact, diplomacy, cool intelligence and quirky sense-of-the-ridiculous was a source of inspiration to many of us during those Le Carré-like days of the early APG.

A great survivor. But, also, Oakley was something of a late developer. *Eugene Flockhart's Desk* was the first play of Barry's to be performed (the version in this collection has been specially re-written for radio). He says he remembers it as vividly as he does the day of his marriage — and for the same reason: he was equally nervous at both! The performance occurred in 1967 at Wal Cherry's Emerald Hill Theatre in South Melbourne. Though little more than a rehearsed reading, it was a big event for the thirty-six-year-old Oakley, who, save for a few stories in obscure magazines, had had nothing published or performed, though *A Wild Ass of a Man* was imminent. He recently described the sensation in a letter headed "Notes and Cribs for Lazy Introducers, Makers of Toasts, Quips etc.":

... My family came along, my friends, and as at my wedding ten years earlier, I wore a blue suit, and felt embarrassed, because the actors and the miniscule audience were in baggy jumpers and jeans. Right on cue the gods, angry perhaps that the theatre was to close for good the following night, organized a deafening rainstorm the moment the play opened so that the reading began as a kind of inert mime: nothing moved except the actors' mouths.

Cherry's Emerald Hill concentrated mainly on European theatre: Moliere; Osborne; Arden; Anouilh ... This was a natural enough emphasis given the absence of good local scripts. However, across town in Carlton another theatre, vigorously Australian in character, was about to replace it — that little old shirt factory called La Mama.

While *Flockhart* was the last play at Emerald Hill, *Witzenhausen* was one of the first at La Mama. Thus Barry, (the only person to work at every new theatre in Melbourne in the past twelve years) a central figure from the beginning, the ageing trendy, was a kind of bridge between the two. However, the two plays are essentially of a pair: absurdist in mode and content, they vent their anger on two kinds of conformism — public service bureaucracy in *Flockhart* and big-business, institutionalization in *Witzenhausen*.

His satire was based on first-hand observation, for, during this period, he was doing time in adjacent cubicles at the Department of Trade and Industry with fellow playwright Ted Neilsen who remembers him in this way: " ... Barry was always different".

At times it was impossible to include him in the conversation. He couldn't drive, didn't own a car and was unconcerned about this implied rejection of peer group priorities.

He carried with him the aura of past encounters with education. Sometimes he was stern and grey — the watchful Brother; at other times, a slyly, wryly joking schoolboy, waiting to be caught.

His profile was a low one.

He had the lowest desk on the fifth floor and had screwed his chair down to match. It was almost as though he didn't want anyone to see the fate that had befallen him.

He seemed to have an embryo-placenta relationship with a round grey rubbish bin close by his right hand. Constantly, his hand would slide amongst the papers of the bin and pull out hidden soul-sustaining pieces of sandwich, fruit and cake.

Someone set fire to his bin one day and after that he changed.

We weren't surprised when, shortly afterwards, he left us to be a Playwright.

Of the other plays in this collection, *Mogadon* (that pill of a play) was commissioned and performed by the ABC. Written in 1979, it returns to the concerns of the first two: the corruption and mesmerism of power, the disparity between the insignificant and the almighty.

Oakley, the all-rounder, the Ian Botham of Australian letters, does not ignore Literature in this collection by any means. *Scanlan* and *The Hollow Tombola* are both literary plays, and in this sense relate in some way to a *Lesson in English* (based on a poem by Marvell) and *The Ship's Whistle* (which used, theatrically, a good deal of the Victorian poetic rhetoric of Richard Orion Horne). *Scanlan* which is a sort of english department *Stretch Of The Imagination* also points to a more personal style for Oakley, relying less on satire and comic exaggeration and more on character observation and compassionate naturalism.

If there are elements of naturalism in *Scanlan*, *Buck Privates* is the only "realistic" play in this truly remarkable writers set of six (or sit of sex) — and what a rib-tickler it is.

As I write this introduction (from Oakley's notes on himself) I am, in fact, in the middle of preparation for the production scheduled for early in 1980 of *Scanlan*, *Buck Privates* and *The Hollow Tombola* for Hoopla at the Playbox, under the collective title: TRICYCLES.

Oakley calls them " . . . these short unplayables of mine" — but I think they may prove as durable as the cultivated and compassionate man who has written them.

Graeme Blundell
August 1979

Acknowledgments

Witzenhausen, Where Are You? was first published in *Meanjin* 2/1967,
Buck Privates in *Nation Review*, 24 November 1977,
and *Scanlan* in *Meanjin* 1/1978.

Witzenhausen, Where Are You?

CHARACTERS AND ORIGINAL CAST

The play was first performed by the Leeton Dramatic Society on 22 August 1967, with the following cast in order of appearance:

KELLY (A Clerk): Frank Bladwell
TYLER (Another Clerk): Laurie Talbot
DANIELSON (A Personnel Manager): Michael Dowd
ARNOLD (A Sales Manager): Maurice Knight
FLUNKEY
CARETAKER
LEADER OF DELEGATION: David Swain
FOUR ASIANS / ATTENDANTS
MARSHALL (A Managing Director): David Rees
WITZENHAUSEN (A Messenger): Stephen Reynolds

Two walls with office doors and a main entrance leading off, converge, but not too obviously, onto a central door at rear, above which is written: MEN. *Company emblem of* COMET MOTORS *on wall.*

Young man in suit enters, goes to door marked MEN, *tries it in vain, waits, whistles, lights cigarette, shows obvious discomfort, paces up and down. Another fellow appears, similarly dressed.*

KELLY (FIRST MAN) : I don't know who's in there, but he's taking one hell of a time.

TYLER (SECOND MAN) : Look here, I can't wait. I can hardly move. I'll have to crawl to the one up the other end.

KELLY : Save your knees. It's out of order. The plumbers are banging away like madmen round there. It's bedlam.

TYLER : Oh God. I'll just have to sneak up to the executives' washroom, that's all. Ever seen the toilet paper they got up there? It's mauve, to go with the tiles. They've got two saunas, a scales, a set of barbells — everything.

KELLY : The executives' washroom? That's forbidden territory. How come you ever made it?

TYLER [*showing obvious signs of discomfort as he talks*] : I was *sent* up once. To get Arnold. A long-distance call from America. I knocked, went in. He was in the steam-room, all pink and flabby and glistening. He looks at me through the mist — those two beady eyes — Boy? What are you doing here? he says. A long-distance call, I say to him — from America. You should've seen him *move* — you'd have thought I'd connected him to a live wire. Jiggling like a frog, trying to get into his suit — out he goes, fly unzipped, hair all over his head, picks up the phone, and you know what he said?

KELLY : No, what?

TYLER : "Yes. Yes. Yes. Right away. Will do." That's all.

KELLY : He said a lot more than that yesterday, I'll bet.

TYLER : Oh sure. Boy, what a convention! You should've been there! Girls, gags, songs, speeches, beer — and every damned Comet dealer in the state. Arnold went mad — he begged, swore, roared, yelled, pleaded with them to sell more Comets. "Y'got to sell those units, I tell you — *y'got* to sell them. Y'got to send your salesmen out roaring like lions for prospects. Y'got to sell! D'you hear me? Sell! Sell! Sell!"

KELLY : He's crazy. They're all crazy. Those cars are just piling up out there behind the factory. They can't give 'em away. People just won't buy! So what do they do? They fire the workers. They kick the men off the line.

TYLER : So what? What else can they do? If they can't sell 'em, what's the use of making them?

KELLY : They go boom — then bust. Boom — then bust. They don't *plan*. It's all too hectic — hey, hurry up in there, for the love of Mike — we're dying out here, come on!

TYLER : There's two waiting, you know. You've had your god-damned smoke and read of the paper — you want us to break down the door? [*To* KELLY] And that's not all. You heard the latest? About Arnold and Witzenhausen?

KELLY : Witzenhausen? The man who carries round the messages? Don't tell me they've come to blows.

TYLER : Well, almost. You know that new dictating machine Arnold's so proud of? Well, he's dictating a memo, see, only about an hour ago it was — and old Witzenhausen comes in, his arms full of papers, his transistor going full blast. Arnold plugs on, dictating his message to all the papers about company retrenchments and drops in sales. "Terrible," says Witzenhausen through his beard — "terrible", he says. "Is there no justice?" "Mind your own goddamned business," says Arnold. "It *is* my business," says this crazy man — it's all on the tape, they've been playing it over and over down in the typists' pool. "*Your* business," says Arnold — you can almost hear him bursting a blood vessel on the tape — "*your* business," says Arnold, "is to clear the outbasket, fill the inbasket, then get the hell out." So out goes the beard, giving the door a bang that almost knocks over the recorder. Old Witz hasn't been sighted since.

KELLY : Good for him. I'm glad someone's got the guts to stand up to him, monster that he is.

TYLER : You can't blame Arnold for being touchy. When sales fall, he's the one that cops it — right in that thick red neck.

KELLY : It's crazy! The big boss puts the pressure on Arnold, he puts the pressure on the dealers, the dealers put the pressure on the salesmen, the salesmen turn the heat on the prospects — and nothing happens! All you can hear on the car lots are the flags flapping — millions of bright plastic flags — flap-flap-flap — the silence is deafening. I say, come on in there for God's sake! Come on!

TYLER : Listen — I can hear music — he's listening to the damned radio in there, so help me.

KELLY : Hey, is the door stuck? Can't you get out? You sick or something? Had a stroke? Gone to sleep?

TYLER : Hello — he's pushing some paper under the door — hey, he's *written* on it — he's written on the damned toilet paper. "The Lord — The Lord Has Made Me His Messenger." That's all it says. "The Lord Has Made Me His Messenger." What d'you make of that?

KELLY : Maybe it's Stollery, the clown from accounts. He's a practical joker from way back — a great ink-blob and rubber spider man. Hey, is that you Stollery? It's a joke, isn't it? Will you please come out? No one out here is laughing — we're in agony, you hear that? Absolutely no one is laughing.

TYLER : That writing — it's sort of scrawled, like a little boy's.

KELLY : Who's in there? Come on, who is it? You in trouble? Need a doctor? Psychiatrist? There's both on the premises. Want us to push you under a laxative?

TYLER : Another message. You got through to him anyway. "Once I Was The Messenger of Men. Not Now." Over and out. That's all.

KELLY : Messenger? Music? I know, I know — it's the man himself. Of course — it's Witzenhausen, the mad messenger. He's locked himself in. Because of Arnold — the row he had with Arnold.

TYLER : Witzenhausen? That you? Why don't you come out? They fired you, is that it? I'm in agony, you fool. I should be back at my desk. They'll send the Gestapo out looking for me any minute.

KELLY : More paper. He's really letting himself go. [*Reads*] "He That Humbleth Himself." That's all it says.

TYLER : He That Humbleth Himself? That doesn't make sense — it's Witzenhausen all right. It figures.

KELLY : He that humbles himself shall be exalted. And he that exalts himself shall be humbled. He's hitting us with a fast bit of scripture. Well, what can we do? Should we tell anyone, or just sit here and die?

TYLER : Well, *I* can't wait, that's for sure. Not a second longer. I'm going up to heaven — to the executives' washroom. If they knock me back there, so help me I'll find myself a quiet corner and a fire-bucket. Maybe you'd better get Danielson, *he's* the Personnel Officer. It's his baby — staff problems and all that. It's part of his job — let *him* work it out.

KELLY : No. That'll only get Witzenhausen into more trouble. He's had brushes with Danielson before. Besides, Danielson's got his hands full trying to keep 'em happy at the plant. How d'you keep eight hundred men happy when they've just been given a week's notice?

[TYLER goes.]

Listen, Witz. It's Kelly — Kelly, you know me? I'm your friend. I've bought you beers, I've listened to your free verse. I liked it Witz, remember? That time we went up on the roof together and you roared it out. I'd hate to see you go, Witz, I mean that. You're different, you break the monotony. Have a bit of sense and come out good and quiet while there's no one around. Honest, I won't tell a soul. If you're fired, who'll I have to talk to? Ever thought of that? Who else'd wear a red velvet jacket into work? Who else'd go into the accountant's office wearing a Frankenstein mask? Come out Witz, while the going's good!

[*Enter* DANIELSON.]

DANIELSON : Morning, Kelly. You talking to yourself?

KELLY : Er no — just waiting, just waiting. The other toilet's being repaired, and there's a bit of a rush on this one. Suddenly everyone decides he wants to — spend a penny.

DANIELSON : You seen them? Have they arrived yet? Any activity at the front door? We're expecting a party of visitors any minute. Asian engineers — here to look over the plant. With a bit of luck, I'll be able to nip in here before they arrive. I've had a bad stomach all morning. Some wog that's going around — quite a few off down at the plant.

KELLY : Oh, it's a wog, is it? I thought it was falling sales.

DANIELSON : Well, what can we do? I mean, if the public won't buy, it's not much use building the car — now is it? It's easy to stand off and criticize, but what do you do?

KELLY : You know what I'd do? I'd give 'em more than a week's notice, for a start.

DANIELSON : Listen — you're just a little tiny voice down the back of the invoice department. This is a business, not a charity organization.

[*A short silence. They sit side by side, gloomy.*]

Hey, hurry up in there will you? There's two waiting! The time they waste in office toilets! Hey, listen — that's music — he's got a radio on in there. What does he think it is, the recreation room? Who's in there, so help me God?

KELLY : It's Witzenhausen.

DANIELSON : Witzenhausen! No wonder he's in hiding. Nothing but trouble ever since we hired him. He'll have to go — he'll really have to go. But hold on — he's pushing something under the bloody door, would you believe it? A damned piece of toilet paper if you please, with writing on it. Here, you read it — I haven't got my glasses.

KELLY [*reads*] : "Management. The Devil's Work."

DANIELSON : Go on, go on.

KELLY : That's all. That's his fourth.

DANIELSON : His fourth what?

KELLY : His fourth message. He's locked himself in. He won't come out.

DANIELSON : He's what? Oh, he's gone too far this time. He's over-stepped the mark. Cooked his goose. We've been tolerant, but this is too much.

KELLY : He had another brush with Mr Arnold, did you know that?

DANIELSON : It's all round the office. That's the trouble with his type. He upsets the place, disturbs company morale. First it was his clothes — that awful red velvet jacket, you remember? Then it was the bottle of wine he brought with his lunch — knowing full well there's no liquor allowed on company premises —

KELLY : What about the board room? The beer, the gin, the whisky? They're loaded with it up there.

DANIELSON : That's different, you ought to know that. That's for entertaining important visitors.

KELLY : They must have a hell of a lot of VIPs. Those boys go through about a crate of Scotch a week.

DANIELSON : You've got the wrong attitude, Kelly. You're always looking for faults, picking the place over, testing it for hidden weaknesses. That's no way to get on, don't you understand that?

KELLY : Yes, I understand that. Perfectly.

DANIELSON : We should never have hired that man. I was against it right from the start. I told them. I showed them his answers in the aptitude test. One of the questions we gave him was: "What would you do if there was a fire in the plant?" You know, it's designed to test initiative. Know what he wrote? "I'd run away," he says. Yes, run away. Not suitable, I told them. Definitely not suitable. But did they take any notice? Not them! Witzenhausen? It's Danielson here, Personnel. I want you to listen to me carefully. Ready? What's the trouble now, come on, what is it? Some inter-office grudge? Some problem in your personal life? A bit of emotional stress? No need to worry — no need to worry at all — it happens to the best of us at times. Listen now — listen — here's my point — you won't solve anything — not a thing — by locking yourself away and hiding. Sometime or other you'll have to come out, you can't stay there forever — you'll have to come out and face up to the facts! The facts! So why not now, eh? Why not now?

KELLY : Come on Witz, I'm in pain out here. I'll go up like a Mills bomb any moment, you hear me? Whatsay you just move over? There's room for two, if you stand.

DANIELSON : There's no need to be flippant about it, you know. You'll only encourage him. Besides, it could be serious. It's a stress situation — the man may be emotionally disturbed. Witzenhausen, now you listen to me. You've got nothing to gain by staying in there. You got a problem? A worry? Something on your mind? I'm your man. You've got professional help right here. That's my job, you know that. Remember when you had your last bit of trouble? Who was it straightened things out? Come on now, who was it?

KELLY : Which bit of trouble, of all the bits?

DANIELSON : When he tried that lunchtime poetry reading session in the canteen — there he was on a table, spouting that crazy stuff through his beard. It was the *workers* who complained, you want to remember that. . . . Witzenhausen! I've tried to be reasonable, done my best to be sympathetic. I'll have to get Mr Arnold, that's all I can do — he'll be in no mood to reason with you, I can assure you of that. Now why don't you call it a day and come out? [*A brief pause.*] God, those Asians'll be here any minute now. I'll be welcoming them, with that crazy lunatic holed up there in the toilet. I'm going to get Arnold. I'd like a second opinion on this one — the man's emotionally disturbed, not a doubt about it.

KELLY : So's Arnold. That's not going to solve anything, now is it? Why not just leave him alone?

DANIELSON: How long have you been here, Kelly? Tell me.

KELLY : Me? Oh, about twelve months — nearer thirteen. Why do you ask?

DANIELSON : When you've been in the world of business a bit longer, you'll understand that things like this just can't be left alone. They spread, like a disease. Company morale, Kelly. It's a fragile thing — and it's fools like Witzenhausen who poison it. Wait here. I'm getting Arnold. If the Asians come, steer them over into the lobby.

[*He goes.*]

KELLY : Listen Witz. It's me, Kelly. I'm all on my own again. Arnold's coming. Come out of there, walk forty paces, open the front door, go straight down the steps and get the hell out. You listening? I know just how you feel. In fact I envy you, I really do. You job's not all that bad, you know. At least you move around the place. Take me — I'm stuck at that one desk, you know, the fifth from the end in row two,

invoices, invoices, invoices, morning till night, a clerk in a
dark suit, surrounded by more clerks in dark suits. We sit at
nine, we relax at ten — a hundred hands reach into a
hundred drawers for Coke bottles and cigarettes, then back
we go again — you hear me Witz? It's inhuman, that's what
it is. But what can we do — we'd need a hundred toilets . . .
[*Re-enter* TYLER.]

TYLER : What, you're still talking to him? I thought there'd be
some action by now. I mean it's the only goddamned toilet
on the floor.

KELLY : Danielson's gone to get Arnold. You know what *he's* like
with big decisions. He's gone for a second opinion, and
here's old Witz with the latest off the presses. [*Reads*]
Listen: "Power is Radioactive. All Need Lead Shields." Not
bad, that. I rather like the way he's put it.

TYLER : Not bad? He's *mad*. Not a shadow of doubt about it.
You've only got to *look* at him. He doesn't belong here. The
crazy New Australian bum. The little showman with the big
beard.

KELLY : Just because he dresses differently? That's the trouble
with these places. There's a proper way to dress for the
office, and a proper way to act and a proper way to write a
business letter. That's why all our desks are the same. We
don't like anyone who's different. We don't like people with
funny clothes or funny walks or funny ideas.

TYLER : He's a bum, and you know it. What is he, thirty? So he
writes crazy poems, and he plugs his ear into his transistor.
He lives in a dream world. All his life he'll take messages
and empty trays — all his life.

KELLY : But he *does* it, doesn't he? And when he doesn't do it,
what happens? Paralysis starts to set in. The first death-
pangs of mighty Comet Motors. Messages aren't collected,
the papers pile up in the trays. The place slowly grinds to a
stop. And look — here's another message from our sponsor.
He's going great — keep it up, Witz — we're rooting for you
out here, all the lousy little underdogs.

TYLER : "The Evil Starts Here. This Office a Microcosm. Fight!"
End of commercial What the hell's a microcosm, an insect?

KELLY : A world — a world in miniature. That's what this place
is. He's on the ball, that Witz. At the bottom, the men in

greasy overalls over at the plant. They're out, they eat on their own, in a special canteen. Then come the clerks in a grey mass. At the top, the men with the hard eyes and the steely voices. He's right. That's the world in a nutshell.

TYLER ; He's crazy.

KELLY : We're crazy, because we don't wear lead shields. If you're big, you get a carpet and a picture window to stop you going mad. If you're small, you get a square of blotter, three drawers, and a date pad. A seat in the third-class compartment. Millions of us, sitting, waiting, travelling to nowhere, regulated by buzzers. I say to hell with it. I say —

TYLER : Look out, they're coming. Watch what you say now, watch what you say.

KELLY [*circumspectly*] : I say, vote Witzenhausen. But quietly.

[*Enter* DANIELSON, ARNOLD.]

ARNOLD : Now look here, I'm right in the middle of a bloody meeting. I've got five of our biggest dealers in there — and you drag me out because that crazy New Australian bastard's locked himself in the can. He belongs in there, the goddam reffo. And he'd better *stay* in there, if he values his life, the way he went on to me this morning — barging in like a one-man band, transistor going full blast, while I'm in the middle of dictating an important message. God, I could have killed him. What is it about that guy? Witzenboom or Witzenlooper or whatever your name is! You listen to me now. I won't fool around with you. I haven't time to waste. It's Arnold here, you hear me? You know who I am, don't you? Witzenblum, I'll give you just ten seconds — you understand? — just ten seconds flat to get the hell out of there — and if you don't you're getting your marching orders. You know what that means? The sack, the boot. Right, I've got my watch on you now — let's see you move — 1-2-3-4-5-6-7-8-9-10 — out! The fight's over, Witzenjammer. You're fired. Finished. You can pack your gear and go. And if you come to us for a reference, you'll get it on toilet paper. . . . Right, let's go. This has gone far enough. We'll get the bugger out, so help me we will —

TYLER : Take it easy Mr Arnold. Remember your blood pressure.

ARNOLD : To hell with my blood pressure! I've had enough of this!

Get the caretaker to bring up his hacksaw right away. We'll
soon have the so-and-so out of his castle.
[*Enter* FLUNKEY.]

FLUNKEY : Mr Arnold, the dealers —

ARNOLD : Okay, okay, I'm coming. Worry, worry, worry — I'm the
one who should be locking himself in. Five thousand new
cars on showroom floors and nobody buying.
[*He goes.*]

KELLY : Wow. I thought he'd blow a gasket.

TYLER : Can you blame him? What happens to the sales
manager when there aren't any sales to manage?

KELLY : When the sales fall, so does the axe. Sudden death for
eight hundred men. What kind of system is that? They go,
not Arnold.

DANIELSON : What d'you mean, what kind of system? Who are you
to talk? An invoice clerk, third grade. That's all you'll ever
be, the way you're talking. Blame the public, they're the
ones who won't buy the cars. It's not our fault.

KELLY : It *is* our fault. It's crazy. We produce too hard, we
advertise too hard, and we do it all with our eyes shut. We
blow up the balloon, and when it goes bang in our faces we
say we can't understand it. Then we fire the guys who make
the car instead of the ones that make the decisions.

TYLER : Are you mad? You want to get fired too?

KELLY : I'm not mad. It's the system that's mad — not me — or
Witzenhausen for that matter.

DANIELSON : No one *makes* you work here Kelly — ever thought of
that?

KELLY : So I leave here, what happens? I go to another desk and
another date pad in some other office. Like the man in the
toilet says, it's everywhere, it's in the air you breathe. You
just can't escape it.
[*Enter* CARETAKER.]

CARETAKER : Now what's this about a door being jammed?

DANIELSON : It's not that it's *jammed*, Jack, it's just that the guy
won't *open* it. Listen Witzenhausen. The caretaker's here,
and he's going to hacksaw straight through that catch. So
you might as well come out — what d'you say?

TYLER : Well, what does he say?

KELLY : Wait on, give him time. Here it comes, here it comes —

"Destroy My Privacy and You Destroy My Life." How about that?

TYLER : Nuts. What's that, some kind of riddle?

KELLY : That's no riddle. He means — at least I think he means — that he's going to kill himself if we force open that door.

TYLER : He wouldn't have the guts. He's all piss and wind. Five feet four of genuine phoney.

DANIELSON : Don't touch that door yet, I've got to think. We may have to get the police. He could become violent. You can never tell with these shifty fellows. They can go right off — just like that. Remember that tall funny guy we had on the assembly line about twelve months ago? MacGill or MacGoo or something. Red hair on top, and a rash of badges all down one side of his overalls. Football club badges, Legacy, Red Cross, Holy Name Society, RSL, Ancient Order of Oddfellows, you name it. One wife, five kids, and as quiet as a mouse. Then one day without warning he ups and has a go at the foreman with the rubber hammer he used to put in the windscreen with. You've got to watch your step with these fellows, I tell you. Listen Witzenhausen, I'll give you one last chance before we call the cops, do you hear me? You're trespassing on company property, but never mind. We'll clear the place. We'll all go away, so nobody'll see you. You can fold up your toilet paper and steal away. What d'you say now, eh?

TYLER : Listen. He's turned the music up. He's communing with the Lord. Put in your money and out comes the Coke bottle. Here she comes! And it's my turn for a read. "800 Workers Fired, And Who Cares? Protest! Protest!"

[*Crash of gong.*]

DANIELSON : My God, here they are! The visiting Orientals! What a time, what a time!

[*Enter Asian delegates, to oriental music, bowing and ceremonious.*]

LEADER OF DELEGATION : Ah so. Take me to your leader, please?

DANIELSON : Welcome, welcome. Danielson's the name, Personnel Manager.

LEADER: Ah. The Manager. In person. What honour! Personal!

[*They all bow.*]

DANIELSON : No, no. The Personnel Manager. Personnel,

Personnel. Welcome, visitors from foreign parts! Here from
distant lands! So much to show you gentlemen! So little
time! Let us proceed!

LEADER [*unrolls a parchment*] : Mister Danielson, manager personally, and fellow representatives of modern Western
technology. It is a pleasure and a privilege for us, humble
visitors from developing countries, to stand before you
today. We are here to learn, we come with eager minds and
trembling cameras. Most profitable we know it will be, this
visit, not only to us as individuals but also to the primitive
lands which we have the dubious honour to represent. Most
valuable, too —

[*Thumping from behind the toilet door.*]

Most valuable too —

DANIELSON : Most valuable, I'm sure. Thank you, gentlemen, for
your well-chosen words. But we can't waste time. Every
minute wasted may mean some vital technical point not
grasped. The plant, the research centre, the executive
offices — so much to show you, we've got to hurry!

LEADER : Excuse me, kindest of sirs. [*Whispers to him.*]

DANIELSON : You what? But of course. At our earliest conve-
nience. Unfortunately this particular one is out of order at
the moment — not functioning — cannot be used.

[*Banging on the door.*]

DANIELSON : That's the plumber, busy at his duties. In the West,
we repair things, you understand. And now, if you'll step
this way, I will take you into Mr Stock, our Works
Manager. He will show you over the plant. I have a small
matter to attend to, and will be following you shortly.
There we are now, through this door now — ah so. First
office on the left.

[*He disappears briefly with the party, then returns. The
others are laughing*]

What the hell are you laughing at? That damned little
bastard in there. Nearly caused an internatonal incident.
I'm winkling the little peanut out of there, so help me.

KELLY : Listen, he's yelling out. He thinks they're still here.
What's that about the men of Asia, Witz? We what? We
should learn from them, not them from us? Ah so, ah so.

DANIELSON : He's rambling. Raving. Get the hacksaw, Jack. I'm calling his bluff. Get going on that lock, and make it snappy.

KELLY : Wait. If he means what he says, he'll kill himself. And *you'll* get the blame, Mr Danielson. The police'll come, and the reporters and the TV crews — and you know how Comet Motors loves publicity. MAN SHOOTS HIMSELF IN COMET TOILET. The newspaper boys'll go mad over this one.

DANIELSON : Wait, wait, hold it Jack. Let's think a minute.

KELLY : He's cunning. See that? Sensing uncertainty in opposition forces, Witzenhausen renews the attack — listen. [*Picking up and reading bit of paper.*] "Managers, Department Heads, Principalities, Powers. No More, No More."

DANIELSON [*shouting*] : The world wouldn't function without leaders, Witzenhausen — you know that. What's he say? Put your ear to the keyhole — he's shouting something back at us.

KELLY [*listening*] : President Johnson, General de Gaulle, Chairman Mao, the Pope — he says he's written to them. All the leaders of the world. Urging them to contemplate. He says he'd like to talk to Mr Marshall.

DANIELSON : Mr Marshall? The managing director? Who does he think he is, God?

KELLY : He's yelling that we must get Marshall quickly. Time is short, so he says.

DANIELSON : It's impossible. Why, I've been here five years, and I've only spoken to Mr Marshall twice in that time.

KELLY : Why is it impossible? He's human, isn't he? Maybe he'll make Witz see reason. It's worth a try.

DANIELSON : Mr Marshall! I wouldn't dare. You'd never get through to him. You've got to pass three secretaries, barking like Alsatian dogs.

KELLY : You're afraid to ask him, is that it?

DANIELSON : Don't be stupid, Kelly. How immature you are. How could you possibly explain it — "Mr Marshall, excuse me, but one of the most insignificant and foolish of all your ten thousand employees has locked himself in the lavatory and won't come out. He'd like a word with you." Now I ask you — how does that sound? What about you, Kelly? You're the one doing all the big talk. Why don't you give it a go?

KELLY : All right, I'll try it. I'm only a clerk, I've got nothing to lose. If I'm not back in five minutes, you'll know I've been eaten alive. God, here I come.
[*He goes.*]

DANIELSON : Can you hear me, Witzenhausen? We're trying to get Mr Marshall for you. It won't be easy, but we're trying. Hold your horses and don't do anything rash . . . don't do anything rash! [*Aside.*] Has Witzenhausen ever done anything else but?
[*Thumpings on door, muffled shouting.*]
Good God, you'd think he was *trapped* in there. What's he saying?

TYLER [*listening*] : He reckons he's free and we're imprisoned and he's trying to figure a way to help us. We're the ones who want to get out, according to him.

DANIELSON : I don't like the sound of this. I'd say he's approaching the flashpoint — he could do anything. We'd better be ready in case he storms out. He could come out firing or wielding a knife. Pull those chairs and tables across and turn 'em over. It might sound funny to you fellows, but I'm the one who's blamed if anything happens. Be prepared, that's my motto. Come on now, build 'em up into a barricade. Then if he rushes us, we'll be ready for him. . . . Wait, what's that? Do I hear trumpets? My God, it's the managing director. Kelly's gone and got the great man himself. Down on your knees, boys. Don't look until you're looked at and keep your powder dry.
[*Enter* MARSHALL, *borne on a kind of litter by company attendants wearing large Comet Motors emblems.*]
Mr Marshall! What have we done to deserve — a personal appearance! To see you in the flesh! Are you ill, sir? Can't you walk?

MARSHALL : At ease. Try to relax. Don't hide your faces, I like to see you all. I wish I could come down here more often, to chat informally with my staff. Yes, I'm ill. A slight stroke has deprived me of the use of my limbs. Thank heavens my decision-making faculties are virtually unimpaired. Now, what seems to be the trouble? You.

DANIELSON : Sir — sir, sir . . .

MARSHALL : Calm down now. Take it quietly. I'm human, just like yourselves, try to realize that. You, perhaps you have a tongue in your head.

KELLY : We have a messenger, sir, a humble emptier of out-trays by the name of — forgive me sir, it sounds grotesque — Witzenhausen. This man has locked himself in the toilet. He refuses to come out. He communicates with us by — if you will pardon the expression — toilet paper. You have heard of the material, my lord? It is not unknown to you?

MARSHALL : Yes, I vaguely remember it from the days of my youth. Proceed, young man. What's your name, by the way? I rather like the way you speak up.

KELLY : Kelly, sir. James Kelly.

MARSHALL : Make a note of it [*to an attendant, who writes in a notebook*] — James Kelly. You may hear from us shortly — don't call us though, we'll call you. I rather like the cut of your jib — continue.

KELLY : Well sir, we've tried everything, we've tried to reason with him, but it's no good — and now he's asking for you.

MARSHALL : Good lord, eh? This is rum. Let me think now — it's hard, hard, staff, this thinking business, since I've had this stroke. Wait a minute, I have it, ah yes — why not, wait, yes, of course, why not off with the door — eh? Off with the door! Thought o' that, hey?

KELLY : But sir, if we touch the door, he's threatened to take his life — take matters into his own hands — terminate his existence.

MARSHALL : What? You mean kill himself?

DANIELSON : Just so, sir. Your perceptions are as rapid as ever, if I may humbly say so. My name is Danielson sir — you know — Personnel — Personnel Manager. Danielson, sir.

MARSHALL : Hmm. Can't place you. Well now, this Witzenblatter wants to see me; I'm here, I'm ready, so what do we do?

DANIELSON : Wait sir, I'll tell him. The shock of your physical presence, in our midst so to speak, may serve to bring the unfortunate man to his senses. [*To* WITZENHAUSEN] Mr Marshall is here, Witzenhausen. Do you understand? Do you realize what a sacrifice this involves on his part? Can you imagine his responsibilities, the urgent matters demanding his attention? Well, he's here. Standing before us now. This is your chance to touch the hem of his garment. Come out now, and quickly.

MARSHALL : Well? What's the matter with the man? I don't hear anything. Not a damned sound.

KELLY : He's probably writing, sir.

MARSHALL : Writing?

KELLY : Yes, sir. As we said, he pushes little written messages under the door.

MARSHALL : Ah yes, yes. Well, let's see what this Witzenrooben comes up with. Ever acted strangely before?

DANIELSON : There was the occasion of the poetry reading in the workers' canteen. Most unfortunate.

MARSHALL : Ah yes. Got us a lot of publicity, that. Good publicity. Bringing culture to the workers kind of thing. Went over very well, I believe.

DANIELSON : Here it comes. ... Oh sir, I don't think — out of respect sir, I'd rather not —

MARSHALL : Come on, come on, let's have it.

DANIELSON [*reads*] : "The More The Power, The Greater The Ailment. This Man Is Ill — But I Can Cure Him."

MARSHALL : Good Lord, how'd he know that? Can he see through that door? Can he hear what we're saying?

KELLY : No sir. Only if we shout.

MARSHALL : He can cure me? Well, you never know. The beggar must have secret powers, you know — telemetry or telescopy — what's the word?

KELLY : Telepathy, sir. Witzenhausen may have psychic powers, you think.

MARSHALL : Well, it's a possibility. What d'you think, Kelly?

KELLY : He may have, sir. He's a remarkable man — very gifted in his own way — artistic, if you follow me, sir.

MARSHALL : Artistic, eh? Psychic, eh? Interesting. You're a smart lad, Kelly. I like a person with a bit of education. You — put an asterisk by Kelly's name, right away. Left school at fourteen myself, and always regretted it. We'll try this Howitzer fellow. Ask him — ask him what I'm thinking about right now. Go on.

KELLY [*shouts*] : Mr Marshall would like you to tell him what he's thinking about at this very moment.

MARSHALL : Yes, yes, I'm thinking hard. I'm trying to get through to him. Very interesting, this mental business. Wonder if he'll pick it up?

KELLY : Oh sir! [*Reads.*]

MARSHALL : Come on, come on, what's he say? Don't hedge man, don't hedge. What *was* I thinking about?

KELLY : Lunch sir. You were thinking about your lunch. See, he's written it down here.

MARSHALL : Goddammit, he's right. I like the sound of this feller. His name's funny, but we could change it into something solid and sensible. Bad for business, a long foreign name. Very bad. I could use this chap at conferences, meetings and the like. Tell him I'm considering him for promotion.

DANIELSON : Promotion sir?

MARSHALL : Promotion! Yes. Go on, tell him. Get a move on, though — I'm starving.

DANIELSON : You're being considered for *promotion*, Witzenhausen, you hear that? By Mr Marshall himself. That'll really knock him over. Hello, the radio's on again. He's going through a crisis. Good tactics, Mr Marshall — I've got to hand it to you. Ah ha, and here's the answer. Didn't take long over this one, did he? Promotion.

KELLY [*reads*] : What's this? "All The Kingdoms Of This World I Will Offer You, If Only You Will Bow Down And Adore."

MARSHALL : What the blazes is he talking about?

KELLY : Scripture, sir. He's fond of Scripture. The time when Lucifer offered Christ the whole world, if only he'd worship him.

MARSHALL : Well I'll be damned. He thinks I'm the devil, does he? It's an idea, anyway. He's got guts, this Witzenblower. We need creative, independent people. Too many yes-men at Comet Motors. That's been the trouble all along. Well, what do we do?

KELLY : He hasn't actually answered your offer, sir. He's probably still enjoying the temptation. Ah see, now we have it. No sir. He says: "No — And Now I Go To The Father". That's his answer.

DANIELSON : Look, there's smoke coming under the door! Behind the barricades! He's going to blow himself up!

MARSHALL : But the cure — ask him — how can he cure me, the blighter. Don't let him get away!

DANIELSON : The music! Explosions! He's going up in flames! Hide!

[*The lights go out, there's a loud bang, the door flies open, revealing a blinding searchlight. A vague dark figure rushes past them with a whoosh, bursts out the front doors, which swing violently. Complete darkness. Shouts of:*]

VOICES : I can't see! I can't see! He's blinded me! The lights won't work! The power's off! Get a torch, a torch! Here, here! A torch! Mr Marshall, Mr Marshall!

MARSHALL : Boys! Boys! I can walk! It's just like one of those sob-stories on the TV! My legs are OK! Get after that man! Bring him back! Don't let him get away!

[*They run to the door.*]

DANIELSON : He's disappeared!

KELLY : It's raining!

TYLER : Gone!

DANIELSON : It's all flat country round here, where could he hide?

MARSHALL : Kibbitzer! Come back! Save us! Save the company! Help!

[*They turn from the door slowly, as the lights go on again, all realizing the toilet is open. In a mob, they rush at it, falling over, fighting, screaming. Only* KELLY *stands apart. After watching them fume and mill at the toilet doorway, he sadly reaches for the switch and turns out the light.*]

END

The Hollow Tombola

A Satire

CHARACTERS

MASTER OF CEREMONIES
WALDO : sharp, clever and old
ARTHUR (WALDO'S TWIN): slow, lumbering and old

A deserted rostrum, readied as if for a lecture. A set of drums.
Enter master of ceremonies in dinner suit. He's dragging a bulky
tarpaulin-covered shape under which are in fact two men, sitting.
He sets the object in position below the rostrum, then ascends to
it. His movements tend to be erratic, nervous — his introductory
speech likewise. After his little speech, when the action begins, he
uses the drums, especially the cymbals and bass, whenever
there's a Significant Moment.

M.C. : This remarkable novel — this achievement — this em-
purpled work — this parable or allegory (I quote from the
front flap) — the symbolism — expressionism — realism —
every ism in the book — even to *talk* of isms is a solecism —
mysticism — lyricism — witticism — catholicism, lower
case (I quote from the back flap) — the front flap and back
flap (*waving his arms as if about to levitate*) — this
fourteen-foot span — this albatross of a novel — soaring
ever higher — over remote seas of the heart — this enigma
for scholars — this cliff at which they quarry endlessly —
chipping away — theme — character — plot — structure —
language — moral concern — this work, which contains
estimated reserves of one million cubic feet — pure natural
gas — enough to power the nation for twenty years. . . . I
bring to you, ladies and gentlemen, the Amazing Tombolas,
direct from Sarsaparilla — Waldo and Arthur — twins —
alike and yet not alike — opposites — enigmas — Waldo
the intellectual — Arthur somewhat strange in the head —
Waldo spare, Arthur ample — Waldo with his writing —
Arthur with his muscles and his mystic marbles. . . . Waldo
Tombola, the hollow Tombola, mean little Waldo, is

ashamed of his big, simple brother — and now they are
going to go out — they are going to leave their overgrown
old house — and go for a walk!

[MASTER OF CEREMONIES *goes down and unveils the
brothers, sitting. One is small and sharp, the other large
and stupid in a mystic kind of way. They sit there,
brooding.*]

WALDO [*turning his head to his brother*] : Time for our walk. . . .
Put on your coat. We'll go for a walk.

[*no reaction.*]

Sitting here brooding. . . . Stop it! Stop that brooding!

ARTHUR [*without moving*] : Brooding. Stop that brooding. Stop.
Stop that brooding.

[*WALDO, exasperated, gets their coats — his an old oilskin,
ARTHUR'S a dingy gaberdine.* WALDO *has trouble getting
ARTHUR'S on because he goes on with his brooding. He puts a
digger's's hat on* ARTHUR'S *head, an old turned-down grey
felt one on his own. Then he calls the two dogs.* MASTER OF
CEREMONIES *makes appropriate dog noises. Dogs become
too frisky.* WALDO *fends them off and abuses them.*]

M.C. : Two men, two dogs. Watch out for objective correlatives.

WALDO : Feel any better?

ARTHUR : Yes Waldo. Better.

WALDO : Indigestion, that's what it is. You swallow too quickly.

ARTHUR : Yes Waldo. Indigestion.

M.C. [*with the brothers enacting what is described*] : Waldo
leads his brother Arthur out of the brown gloom of the
kitchen. Waldo could feel his brother's large fleshy hand in
his thinner colder one as they stumbled in and out of the
grass down what remained of the brick path. His brother
was breathing deeply, Waldo saw.

ARTHUR : Which direction, Waldo?

WALDO : There's only one.

ARTHUR : But after Terminus Road?

WALDO [*impatiently*] : After Terminus Road — the main road.
In the direction of — Barranugli.

ARTHUR : Barranugli — an Aboriginal word?

WALDO : A symbolic word. Barren and ugly. You follow? You get
it?

[*Arthur looks blank.*]

[*Impatient*] : The Council calls it Barranugli. It's Aboriginal — and highly appropriate.

ARTHUR [*shakes his head*] : Don't get it. No understand.

WALDO : Barranugli! Barren! Ugly!

ARTHUR [*not convinced still*] : Ah yes.

M.C. : Sometimes Waldo would look at his brother and try to remember when he had first been saddled with him. He watched him blow out his red, fleshy, but to no extent sensual lips.

ARTHUR [*blowing out his lips*] : Why the main road?

WALDO [*angrily*] : Because I want to see life. Life! Life! You don't want to deny me that?

ARTHUR [*subdued*] : No, Waldo. Keep your voice down.

M.C. : Waldo was punctured then —

WALDO [*hissing, miming puncture*] : S-s-s-s.

M.C. : — but continued on, a thin man in a turned-down stiff grey hat.

ARTHUR : I like the *side* roads. You can look at the fennel.

WALDO [*preoccupied, not hearing properly*] : When they're on houses, dumbchuck, they're chimneys, not funnels.

ARTHUR : Fennel?

WALDO : Funnel.

ARTHUR : Fennel!

WALDO : Funnel!

ARTHUR : I'm not talking about funnels! Women have funnels.

WALDO [*whacking him across face*] : You pretend to be a saint, a simple-mind, and you get away with murder. I won't have loose talk.

M.C. : Arthur had difficulty with words, chewing them to eject —

ARTHUR [*chewing, then spitting*] : Fennel.

M.C. : — but when he did, there they stood, solid and for ever.

[WALDO *grinds the spat-out word with his heel.*]

M.C. [*the brothers mime it all*] : On the broken path, Waldo's oilskin went slithering past the gooseberry bushes. The wind might have cut their skins if they hadn't been protected by their thoughts ... sidling brittly to negotiate the irregular bricks, now pushing Arthur and staring fascinated into his brother's hair, at the glimpses of pale skin beyond. Arthur was still big and strong. His muscles at least had remained youthful.

ARTHUR : This gate, Waldo, will fall to pieces any day now.
WALDO : This gate will outlast us both.
ARTHUR : This gate —
WALDO : Outlast —
ARTHUR : Us both. This gate —
WALDO : Enough! Try not to repeat everything I say.
M.C. : Waldo took his brother by the hand as they entered Terminus Road.
ARTHUR [*expectant, almost lascivious*] : Perhaps if we hang around she'll come out.
WALDO : Who'll come out? Who?
ARTHUR : Mrs Poulter, that's who.
WALDO : Mrs Poulter! Already I'm tired, with your silly talk!
M.C. : Waldo's thin male steps crunched. He walked primly, in the sound of his oilskin, planning in advance where to put his feet . . . whereas Arthur was not exactly running, but lumbering and squelching, while some distress, of feminine origin, was fluttering in his big old-man's body.
ARTHUR : I wonder why Mrs Poulter is so awful.
WALDO : I didn't say she's awful!
ARTHUR : If you don't say it, it's likely to fester.
WALDO : If I want one of your crackerbarrel philosopher mystic insights, I'll ask for it.
M.C. : The two old dogs were having a whale of a time amongst the fresh cow turds and buffalo grass.
ARTHUR : You ought to write about Mrs Saporta.
WALDO : Why Mrs Saporta, for God's sake?
ARTHUR : I saw them.
WALDO : When?
        [*No answer.*]
        When? When?
ARTHUR : Some time ago, I think.
M.C.: Waldo averted his gaze from something. Then he said, from between his original teeth in his cold, clear, articulate tone:
WALDO : I don't want to think or write about the Saportas!
M.C. : Lady callers had enquired about Waldo's writing as though it had been an illness.
ARTHUR ; Well, if you ask me, simple people are somehow —
M.C. : Groping for the word, he formed his lips into a trumpet.
ARTHUR : — somehow more [*trumpeting*] transparent!

M.C. : He didn't shout, but Waldo was deafened by it.

WALDO : More transparent?

M.C. : He hated it. He could have thrown away the fat parcel of his brother's hand.

WALDO : What do *you* know?

M.C. : Waldo was worrying it with his teeth.

WALDO [*worrying it*] : But you were always good at figures, I'll admit that. At figures you were always good.

ARTHUR : Good. At figures. Always. I.

M.C. : Waldo was striding now — the great gates of his creaking oilskin had opened on his narrow chest and the long legs stuffed in gumboots. His flies were spattered in fat from a remote occasion at the stove.

WALDO : With me, it's words. So much I have to express! So much to be done!

M.C. : The heavy Arthur had to run to keep up with his brother. He was whimpering, too. And blubbering.

ARTHUR [*doing both*] : Don't worry, Waldo! There's time, there's still time. You can write about Mr Saporta and the carpets and all the fennel down the side roads.

WALDO : In the fennel lies the funnel,
    Below the earth, there's the gunwale.
See? Poetry. Modern poetry. Stuff you can't understand.

ARTHUR : One of the carpets —

M.C. : Arthur whimpered.

ARTHUR : — had, right in the centre, what I would say was a tombola.

WALDO : Mandala!

ARTHUR : A tombola, one of the carpets had. Is that a symbol, Waldo? What's a symbol?

WALDO : Symbols are what you fill books with. When I write my book, it's going to be stuffed with symbols. They'll pop out the moment you open it. Everything will have a double meaning and no meaning. Come on!

M.C. : He hated his brother . . . . The brothers had almost emerged from the clotted paddocks of Terminus Road into the world where people lived, not the Poulters or themselves but families in advertised clothes who belonged to fellowships and lodges and were not afraid of electrical gadgets. Waldo yearned secretly for the brick boxes to an extent where his love had become hatred .... Now, when he heard his own breathing united with Arthur's and realized how it might startle a stranger, he thought it better to advise —

WALDO : When I said not to brood, I meant *not to brood.*

M.C. : Arthur trotted a little, the white hair flopping at his neck. Waldo freed his hand for a moment. The wind getting in behind his spectacles had stung his rather pale eyes. . . .
[*They both remove clothes to reveal boys' knicker-bockers.*]
It was so many years, he realized, since he had looked at himself without his glasses. He could barely see his youth's face. . . . years ago, when they were building the house, Dad announced, "I know it's no more than a weatherboard, but I want to suggest, above the front veranda, something of the shape of a Greek pediment . . . don't you see? Don't you understand? A pediment — in the classical style." . . . Nobody understood. "Good-oh, Mr Tombola," Mr Haynes said helpfully at last, after it had grown embarrassing. "We'll make yer happy. A Greek impediment you want, a Greek impediment you get." . . . So the classical pediment rose by degrees, above the normal weatherboard, giving it the appearance of an apologetic little temple, standing on the trampled grass . . . . It was Waldo who disturbed the peace —

WALDO [*young, piping voice*] : I'm thinking of writing a play. It's going to be a Greek tragedy.

M.C. : Dad raised his voice as if scenting an approach. "How? You've never seen one or read one." Waldo began to sidle. [WALDO *moving oddly sideways.*] He was never easily carried away.

WALDO : I'll write it. Afterwards I'll act it. Here on the veranda.

M.C. : Then Arthur, who had come up carrying a full pail, halted and started gulping for words.

ARTHUR [*gulping*] : Waldo — I can act in your play, can't I?

WALDO : No.

ARTHUR : Oh, well, I'll write one myself then. It will be about —

WALDO : It will be about what?

ARTHUR : It will be about — a cow. A big yellow cow. She's all blown out, see, with her calf. Then she has the calf — and it's dead. The calf's dead.

M.C. : There was Arthur pawing at the boards of the veranda. At the shiny parcel of dead calf. Everyone was looking at the ground now, from shame, or from terror. Arthur started lowing —

ARTHUR [*lowing*] : You can see she's upset — the cow — can't help feeling upset. Can't help it — feeling upset — the cow.

M.C. : Thundering up and down the veranda, he raised his curved yellow horns, his thick fleshy awful muzzle. The whole framework of their stage shook. "That's enough!" said Dad. [*They put on their old men's clothes again — while* MASTER OF CEREMONIES *proceeds — but also attempt to mime the actions described at the same time.*]

M.C. : Lost in memories, the old men weave along the main street, the one stalking, the other slumping, past the concrete kerbing, the council-approved parapets. The old men were still fascinated by what they knew, while often over-whelmed by it. Especially Woolworths. Arthur loved Woolworths.

ARTHUR : Can't we go into Woolies, Waldo?

WALDO : It isn't open yet, dumbchuck.

M.C. : Arthur liked to spend mornings in Woolworths costing the goods. Once the manager had searched his pockets, and found the bus tickets, the grey handkerchief, and the glass taws he carried around. "Those are my solid tombolas," Arthur explained to the manager. Gathered by the wind, they flitted across the plate glass, each examining himself secretly. Intellectual honesty glittered on Waldo's glasses, blinding his rather pale eyes. But — where was Arthur?

ARTHUR : Look Waldo, it's turned to clay!

M.C. : — Arthur called, fascinated by the crumbling turd of Mr Hepple's over-stuffed cocker spaniel.

WALDO : Come along, you fool. It's only old. Old! Old!

M.C. : Each of the blue dogs, pointing a swivel nose, sniffed with a delicacy of attention, lifted a leg in turn, aimed sturdily enough, then came on, chests broad to the wind. It was Arthur who lingered, as though unable to decide on the next attitude to adopt. Then he spat or dribbled.

ARTHUR : That sort of smell could give a person diphtheria.

WALDO : Didn't I tell you to come along?

M.C. : He took his brother by the hand. They were walking in the direction Waldo knew he had not chosen. It had chosen him.

ARTHUR : Did you ever have diphtheria, Waldo?

WALDO : You know perfectly well I didn't . . . idiot.

ARTHUR : Yes.

M.C. : The habit of motion, the warmth of skin, were so comfortable Arthur put out his tongue and licked the air. It might have been barley sugar.

ARTHUR : You know when you are ill, really ill, pneumonia — you can get —you can get much further in.

WALDO [*irritably*] : Into what?

ARTHUR : Into anything.

M.C. : The wind came round the corner and gave Waldo Tombola the staggers.

ARTHUR : One day I'll be able to explain — make you see. Words are not what make you see. See?

WALDO : I was taught they were.

ARTHUR : I forget what I was taught. I only remember what I've learned.

M.C. : If he stumbled at that point it was because he had turned his right toe in.

[ARTHUR *falls over.*]

ARTHUR : Mrs Poulter said —

WALDO [*with contempt*] : Mrs Poulter!

M.C. : Waldo yanked at the oblivious hand. Mrs Poulter was one of the fifty-seven things he hated. The little flat sounds that accompany dangerous approaches were issuing from Waldo's mouth.

ARTHUR : I don't understand how they can nail a person through the hands.

WALDO [*dragging him along*] : The religious kick, I knew it. Back we go, before you make a total fool of yourself.

M.C. : Then they were walking somewhat quicker, rocking in fact, in an effort to gather speed, or avoid reflections. One of the dogs looked back over his shoulder to see what the men could be getting up to. His splather of tongue hung, palpitating, against the yellow stumps and bleeding gums. When Arthur, as though in sympathy with the dog, held up his thick white muzzle and began to howl.

ARTHUR : Aaaaah! I never went on such a walk! What's it leading
to? Yow-ooooh!

WALDO : Home, that's where it's leading to. And stop your
damned yowling.

ARTHUR : Home?

WALDO : Home.

ARTHUR : Again?

WALDO : Again.

M.C. : And jerked his brother again, so that Arthur was trotting
like a dog, while Waldo strode on long legs, the loosened
sheets of his oilskin chattering in the wind, his shod heels
gashing the stones. At times the brothers reeled. When the
flap of Waldo's oilskin struck the driver's door of the semi-
trailer lurching past, it brought a man rushing out of the
garden of one of the homes. "Steady on," he hollered.
"You'll get hit and *I'll* have to call the ambulance."

ARTHUR : Oh no! Not the ambulance! Not the green cart, and not
the ambulance!

WALDO [*to the man*] : Thank you my friend. We're in full control
of ourselves. [*To* ARTHUR, *hissing*] Get home! Dumbchuck!
Home!

ARTHUR : Home!

WALDO : Don't repeat everything I say.

ARTHUR : Repeat! Everything! No!

WALDO : Here we are, then.

ARTHUR : Then are we here!

WALDO : That's better!

ARTHUR : Or worse!

WALDO : Oh, make the bread and milk.

ARTHUR : What, the moment we get home?

WALDO : The bread! The milk! Come on!

ARTHUR [*starting to prepare it*] : Have you ever been — in love?

WALDO : Meal, meal — not metaphysics!

ARTHUR : I just wondered.

WALDO : What a thing to ask.

ARTHUR : If we loved enough —

WALDO : I'm hungry, you poor fool. Don't, oh simple wits, preach
sermons to me. Your place is in the kitchen.

ARTHUR : The kitchen of the heart.

WALDO : The heart of the kitchen. At the stove!

ARTHUR : Love —

WALDO : Don't say that word, d'you hear? It upsets me.

ARTHUR [*advancing on him with overpowering affection*] : Love — the mystery at the heart of the tombola.

WALDO [*fending him off*] : Back! Back, you fool!

ARTHUR : I see into the tombola's heart — we must love one another! [*Almost crushing him to death.*]

WALDO : You're mad, that's what you are! Mad!

[WALDO *tries to strangle* ARTHUR *to defend himself against his advances. They have a strange grapple, each seeming to strangle the other, while they emit significant words.*]

ARTHUR : Love!

WALDO : Hate!

ARTHUR : Hunger.

WALDO : Bread and milk!

ARTHUR : Life!

WALDO : Nothingness!

ARTHUR : Mystery!

WALDO : Common sense!

ARTHUR : You're hurting me, Waldo.

WALDO : Must keep —

ARTHUR : — in full control —

WALDO : — of ourselves.

ARTHUR : Have to —

WALDO : — do this

ARTHUR : — it's fated.

WALDO : — destined.

ARTHUR : — decreed.

WALDO : — the symbolism.

ARTHUR : — the weight of it. I kill —

[WALDO *expires.* ARTHUR *gets up. Stunned. Arms out like Frankenstein, he mounts the rostrum, while the* MASTER OF CEREMONIES *proceeds.*]

M.C. : Significance — import — profundity — reverberations — blow your nose, Arthur — Arthur, blow your nose —

[ARTHUR *pauses in his advance towards* MASTER OF CEREMONIES *to blow his nose, the tombola falling out of his pocket as he pulls out the dirty handkerchief.*]

ARTHUR : My tombola — I've lost my tombola!

[*He looks around bewildered.*]

M.C. [*nervously*] : Find your tombola, Arthur. Find your
    tombola!
ARTHUR [*looking around momentarily as if lost*] : It's gone, my
    tombola. I kill —
    [*Advances on* MASTER OF CEREMONIES *and strangles him.
    Then sits at his place, takes large bass drumstick, and
    whacks himself on the head with it. Blackout.*]

Buck Privates

CHARACTERS

LOVELOCK: a publicity officer around forty
DALEY: a priest, also around forty

The idea of a middle-class Australian living-room rather than the actuality. The barest furniture essentials: lamp, phone on stand, two chairs, liquor table, stereo, door. The lamp's on. LOVELOCK *comes on suddenly, in pyjama pants and shirt, hurries to phone, dials.*

LOVELOCK : Hello? Sorry to bother you again, my name is Lovelock. I am the gentleman who rang a few minutes ago asking for Father Daley.... Yes, madam, I'm sorry, it was a *distress* call, someone in need of assistance — has he left yet? .... I see. The point is, he's not *needed* any more..... Yes, I realize it's too late now. [*Pause, as he takes a blast.*] I don't want a tirade, madam, there's no need to go on like that.... No, I did not know that you were in bed or that Father has an early mass in the morning.... I *know* the housekeeper's lot is not any easy one, believe me. [*Pause.*] Oh, go to hell!
[*Slams phone down.*]
Harpy! Virago! Termagant! ... Oh God, he'll be here any minute. Hide! ... Lock the doors! ... Draw the drapes!
[*Rushing about*] You fool! Idiot! Blockhead! [*Pause.*] The lights! ... Pretend I'm not at home ... wrong address ... wires crossed ... You and your drunken depressions!
[*He peers round drape, then hides. A pause, during which we hear him mumbling to himself self-accusingly. Sound of car.*]
Oh God, here he comes.
[*Appropriate noises off. Bell rings.* LOVELOCK *lies low. Silence, save for his quiet, self-pitying mumbles. Bell rings*

again. More silence. After a pause, unable to bear the suspense, LOVELOCK *creeps to the window, moves the drape a fraction, peeps very carefully — obviously encountering his visitor's face immediately on the other side of the glass.*]
[*Shocked*] Oh! [*Sickly*] Aha. [*Trying to recover the situation, loudly, through the glass*] So there you are. Coming. Coming.
[*He gets up, goes to door, talking accusingly to himself all the while.*]
Trapped! You fool, you clown, you idiot! What'll I do? What'll I say to the man? It's years, nothing in common, this is ridiculous.
[*Opens door.*]
Aha.

DALEY[*sarcastically, aware of the situation*] : You *are* at home, after all.

LOVELOCK [*embarrassed*] : Yes, I'm at home. . . . Sorry.

DALEY : You ring up someone you haven't seen for years at ten o'clock at night, tell him you're desperate, it's urgent, then when I drive across town at sixty miles an hour you pretend you're not at home. If you *have* decided against cutting your throat I'll do it for you.

LOVELOCK : These things go in waves! You fluctuate! When I rang you, I was way down — right down to rock bottom.

DALEY : If I hadn't've caught you at the window, you'd have let me turn around and drive all the way back again — for nothing.

LOVELOCK : Unforgiveable. But you're in the forgiving businesses.
[*Pause*]

DALEY : Well, which is it? The consolations of the Christian faith, or the door?

LOVELOCK [*getting glasses, whisky*] : Stay, stay — and I'll introduce you to my best friend, Johnnie Walker. Water?

DALEY [*softening, but still resentful*] : Okay, water.

LOVELOCK [*reciting, as he pours the water*] : Veni sanctificator omnipotens deus et benedic hoc sacrificium, tuo sancto nomini praeparatum.
[*Making sign of cross in blessing as he recites.*] Word perfect.

DALEY [*tersely*] : Right words, wrong language. It's in English now.

LOVELOCK : Shows how long since *I've* been to mass.... Five years, to be exact.... Each Sunday missed, a mortal sin.... Five by fifty-two.... Two hundred and sixty sins.... I've got more holes and stains in there than an archery target.[*Intones*] Dominus vobiscum ... et cum spiritu tuo. [*Sighs*] Midnight mass — the choir, the candles, the incense up your nose — and Father Durkin going down on one knee before the consecration [*demonstrating*] and slowly toppling sideways.

DALEY [*still terse*] : He was seventy-two!

LOVELOCK : He was drunk. [*Gets up again*] Remember that competition we had about who could stay down on one knee the longest during the angelus? [*Intones*] And the Word was made flesh and dwelt among us. ... O'Brien won it. Stayed down right till the end of the prayer.

DALEY: And then rose with amazing speed as Brother Myers commenced cuffing him over the head.

LOVELOCK : Sadistic old bastard. [*Imitating Myers.*] Hands up those boys who want saveloys at the school sports.
[*Counts round the class, then stops suddenly.*]
I say, Jones. ... Come up here Pat Jones. ... Why did you have both hands up, Jones? [*Imitating Jones.*] Please sir, I want two saveloys. [*Imitating Myers.*] Whoom! ... Right across the face. ... I got a fleck of poor Pat Jones's saliva on the cheek as it sped across the room.

DALEY [*exasperated*] : That was thirty bloody years ago. Things aren't like that any more.

LOVELOCK : That's no consolation to me. I went to school then, not now. I was plasticine — and mad old Brother Myers moulded me with his huge Hibernian hands. Ten years. The best years of your life. Spent with only one thought in the head. Self-preservation and getting through the period, getting through the day.

DALEY [*incredulous*] : You're not going to blame your failures on the Christian Brothers!

LOVELOCK : I'm a failure, am I? Quick on the uptake, aren't you? There's a man who knows human nature.

DALEY : You said on the phone you didn't want to go on liviing any more. Isn't that some kind of failure?

LOVELOCK : Maybe it's life's fault. Maybe life's failed me. I've had bad luck with jobs and bad luck with women. God hasn't been very kind to me. He's rejected me, so I've rejected him. ... [*Imitating radio announcer.*] Finland has broken off diplomatic relations with Great Britain — BBC news, April 1941... and I've done the same with him [*pointing upwards*]... broken off diplomatic relations ... snap! just like a Violet Crumble.... We don't recognize each other any more.

DALEY : That's because you've forgotten what he looks like. For you, he's a big handball-playing Irishman with a strap sticking out of his habit — and it's all his fault. And that's why you rang me up — you think I'm his local representative.

LOVELOCK : I wanted to talk to someone.

DALEY : Why me? Last time we met you pretended not to know me.

LOVELOCK : You know why? Couldn't bear the way you were walking. You weren't walking up Bourke Street, you were striding up — as if you owned the entire central business district. You were on your way up and I, as usual, was on my way down.

DALEY : Heading for the top, am I? Becalmed by the bay at Middle Brighton — catamaran country, outboard — motorland — beer, barbecues and bikinis — brown skins and blue eyes — and behind 'em — nothing.

LOVELOCK: Amen, I say to you, before you're fifty you'll be a bishop. You've got confidence, personality, and organizing ability. Who could forget how, at the age of eleven, you reorganized the Black Hand Gang — deposing its leader, changing the secret code, and introducing more sophisticated military equipment? Light, portable pea-shooters.

DALEY: I won't be a bishop, and you won't be any different either — a lapsed Catholic and a fervent, practising alcoholic.

LOVELOCK: Exactly. I'll be what I am now. Assistant publicity officer to the Dried Fruits Marketing Board, with a boss ten years younger than I am. I'll still be writing copy for cookery books and school projects.... I'll let you into a little secret. Australian dried fruits contain fifteen per cent more lactose and fructose than dried fruits from other countries — so don't go fooling around with foreign sultanas.

DALEY: I'm not interested in lactose and fructose. I'm tired and I want to go home.

LOVELOCK [*tossing him a packet of dried fruits*] : Then lactose and fructose are just what you want. Energy-giving natural fruit sugars. Go together, like Abbott and Costello. I'll let you into another little secret. I drink on the job. By the time I'm fifty I'll look like a sultana. ... He who lives by the grape dies by the grape. .... Claret at lunchtime and whisky after hours.

DALEY : Look, I really must be going.

LOVELOCK : Of course, it's after hours for you, isn't it? Problems, problems. You get enough of it during the day — without driving over to Blackburn for more.

DALEY : That's right. I'm tired. I rose at six thirty, said Mass to a congregation of three, took Christ into the classroom at the local technical school at nine, said my office, chaired a meeting of the Catholic Women's Social Guild, where we discussed floral arrangements for the altar for the coming week, had lunch, then spent two hours in the confessional listening to stories of lust, masturbation, French kissing, adultery, unnatural acts, and shoplifting.

LOVELOCK [*with irony*] : Rebel! That's what I plan to do. Release white mice at marketing meetings! Bury the general manager in currants! Rape the tea lady and piss in her urn! Hang on, don't go. There's one thing you haven't done. You haven't asked me, about Joy. I've asked you about God, but you haven't asked me about Joy. I know why.

DALEY : Because you'd tell me.

LOVELOCK : Exactly.

DALEY : You're separated?

LOVELOCK : Only for the weekend, unfortunately. Joy has tired of yoga, macrobiotic foods and macrame and is now into amateur theatre. Joy is in Wagga at the amateur drama festival with the Blackburn drama group. Joy is the female lead in *Pygmalion*. Professor Higgins is at this moment attempting the impossible. ... Catherine's away too, because she can't bear the two of us bickering all the time. Bicker, bicker, bicker. That's all we do, Joy and I. Bicker, bicker, bicker. Silly word, bicker. Reminds me of Mr Bickham. Bickham's tennis courts. I liked tennis. Me beating you 6-4, 6-4 on cracked asphalt with the sidelines disappearing into the long grass. Long rallies on warm January mornings.

DALEY : You at the baseline — always at the baseline. And me impatient and storming the net. That's something you've never done.

LOVELOCK : Aha! Move out and meet the ball of life head on, be aggressive, get in there and volley —

DALEY : You let things happen to you. You've always done it.

LOVELOCK : Instead of using my feet to the bowling! Listen, I left the crease once, and I got Joy. Another attacking stroke — and I'm knee deep in sultanas.

DALEY : No wonder the Black Hand Gang was ripe for the taking — with a leader like that. You'd built a series of defensive holes in your front garden expecting the enemy to come to you —

LOVELOCK : *You* were the enemy! The Black Hand Gang was an amiable shambles until you came into the district in 1941 — it wasn't even your territory, you were on the more genteel North Caulfield side of Orrong Road — but you crossed the border, moved in and Pearl Harboured me — you got me down in the aniseed weeds in front of all my men and seized power — and goddammit you've had it ever since.

DALEY : So it's not God or the Christian Brothers then — it's me.

LOVELOCK : You sapped the lactose and the fructose out of me all the way through secondary school — all you left me with was the Christian Doctrine prize.... [*Imitating an announcement.*] And the Senator Keane prize for Christian Doctrine goes to Master Lovelock.
[*Changes character — mimes himself as a schoolboy coming up on the stage overawed, tripping on to his hands and knees.*]
That was another time I ventured out of the crease. Right

over the microphone cord and almost on top of Archbishop Mannix.

DALEY : Tanglefoot Lovelock — the kid they couldn't teach to dance. Dancing lessons on the school handball court from the effeminate Mr Duff: Stick at it, boys, he says, as we waltz over the cracked concrete. Once you've mastered the art, you'll want to go dancing eight nights a week . . . but there is one boy who will never master the art, and I will mention no names — this boy could not win a dancing prize at the Limbless Soldiers' Association.

LOVELOCK : What a year! "Rum and Coca Cola" was top of the pops, Ron Folmer beat Peter Samuel for the title of school bully, Brother Coughlan banned running in the park, Mr Ward told us not to use Vegemite in our sandwiches because Sanitarium foods were Seventh Day Adventist, Brother Anglin wrote a new school war cry — Hurrawin, Wurrawin, Wewhy, Gunnawin — mad Jimmy Franklin took to wandering the classroom on all fours under our legs like a submarine, Dan Hardy conducted us in singing lessons using a ruler with different kinds of Australian timbers in it, and whose life were we studying in Christian Doctrine classes? Blessed Oliver Plunkett!

DALEY : You're still behind the times! He's been canonized!

LOVELOCK : Plunkett? A saint? And you a parish priest — everyone's getting promoted except me. Hey, Brother Dowd asking poor dumb Alec Seymour the meaning of canonization: Out with it my son, out with it — Please sir, it means being shot out of the barrel of a gun. Three of the best — Dowd thought he was trying to be funny. Or the time the said Seymour was asked to put the phrase the good sailor into Latin? Bonga sailora, he said. Bonga sailora. . . . I'm boring you.

DALEY : I'll have to go *home*.

LOVELOCK : You're lucky you've got one.

DALEY : Home's a cold, draughty presbytery with linoleum, plastic flowers and two maiden ladies — a menopausal housekeeper with a moustache and Our Lady of Fatima in blue and white barley sugar on the mantelpiece.

LOVELOCK [*imitating a brother*] : Boys, President Truman regarded Fatima as the greatest event of the century — and he was a Baptist. [*Resumes normal voice*] All right, you tell me *your* problems.

DALEY : I don't want to talk about my problems.

LOVELOCK : Oh no, not in front of the layman — that'd be letting the side down — reversing the order of nature. We take our problems to the clergy and the clergy take theirs to God. I know what your problem is, anyway. Extracting yourself from this embarrassing evening as soon as you see an opening.

DALEY : That's because you're beyond saving. It's not alcohol you're drowning in, it's self-pity. You are God's own whingeing Irishman.

LOVELOCK : That's good, that's what I brought you over for. Sock it to me — straight from the shoulder.

DALEY : You dragged me here to take me with you — you weren't going to drown on your own, not you.

LOVELOCK : Fifty marks to that boy! You are tantamount to a beneficent deity! Mad Brother Myers, reading your prize-winning essay on hydro-electricity to an impressed class, pausing to savor one of your choicer literary flights [*imitating*]: "We could almost say, such are its benefits, that irrigation is tantamount to a beneficent deity — why can't you other chaps write like that?" My essay, of course, on an air raid, came in a poor second — "searchlights like ghostly white fingers probed the London sky". All that literary talent wasted on sultanas!
[*Pause.*]
It's the afternoons that kill me. After lunch it's two a.m. by the office clock — the dark night of the soul, under the flourescent lights.

DALEY : How many out of work — three hundred thousand? And you with your easy, well-paid nine to five.

LOVELOCK : Man can't live by dried fruits alone. I can't wait for five o'clock to come — and when it does, there's nothing. I drive home to central Australia! And you know what happens in a desert from your intermediate geography. Things grow just below the sand, and that's what's happening to me. I've got a tapeworm in there, a star boarder, and no amount of alcohol will flush it out.

DALEY : You cultivate it, like a mushroom in the cellar. Your job's dead, your marriage? — then leave. Walk out of the cemetery.

LOVELOCK : Where to? A room with kitchenette in Fitzroy? I'm yoked to that woman for good. It was you that said the magic words — you married us! You mumbled, you gestured hypnotically, the Araldite did its deadly work, and we limped down the aisle — Siamese twins forever. When you married in the fifties you did it for keeps. A flower in the buttonhole, one white glove, and a new single-breaster from the Leviathan.

DALEY : Separate! Another job, another city!

LOVELOCK : There is no other city! The only city is in here. I carry it round with me.

DALEY : Lovelock. You're well named. A lover of locks. Break'em open!

LOVELOCK : Stop sounding like Norman Vincent Peale!

DALEY : Or Donald Culross Peattie!

LOVELOCK : Or How to Increase Your Word Power.

DALEY : Or the Most Unforgettable Characters I've Met!

LOVELOCK : "The Human Heart, Nature's Miracle Pump". by Paul de Kruif — between the ages of thirteen and eighteen, I must have consumed ten thousand *Readers Digests*. I learned about the male penis and the female vagina from the *Digest*. Didn't get the facts right till I was thirteen.

DALEY : You were probably the only twelve-year-old in the world who believed that the only way human beings copulated was dog fashion. I can still remember your look of disbelief when I informed you about the missionary position. What? you said, almost falling off your Malvern Star — you don't mean to tell me they do it face to face?

LOVELOCK [*intoning in priestly fashion*] : "And Judah said unto Onan, go in unto thy brother's wife, and marry her, and raise up seed to thy brother. And Onan knew that the seed should not be his, and it came to pass, when he went in unto his brother's wife, that he spilled it on the ground, lest he should give seed to his brother. And the thing which he did displeased the Lord: wherefore he slew him" — you taught me about that as well.

DALEY : I did not.

LOVELOCK : Oh yes you did. Listen Lovelock, you said, if you rub it and rub it you'll get a funny feeling and the seed will come out. So I tried, expecting a tiny seed to emerge, like an orange pip, but nothing happened. I was a late developer, held back, amongst other things, by an unrequited passion for your person.

[*Daley gets up suddenly.*]

LOVELOCK : Don't be alarmed. Can't say it would appeal to me at the moment.

DALEY : I'd better go anyway.

LOVELOCK : Biggles Flies West.

DALEY : It's half eleven.

LOVELOCK : Biggles' African Adventure.

DALEY [*exasperated*] : I've got early mass!

LOVELOCK : Biggles, Scourge of the Swastika.

DALEY : We've both had too much to drink!

LOVELOCK [*imitating*] : A tongue of flame from the riddled fuselage licked hungrily along the fabric. Within minutes the entire machine was a — blazing inferno! It's your fault, reverend, you shot me down! Crawled away from the wreckage and married the wrong woman.

DALEY : I was waiting for that. I knew it was coming.

LOVELOCK : Out of the blazing aircraft! While there's time! [*Shows him the door.*]

DALEY[*refusing to leave*] : It was my fault you married the wrong woman? That's the myth that's fed you all these years? Paydirt at last!

LOVELOCK [*imitating their lady elocution teacher*] : Underneath this rich soil there is oil. A tall lady asked me the right time. Watch those vowel sounds boys, don't make them singsong. Master Lovelock, is that you being heedless and silly?

DALEY : You are being heedless and silly.

LOVELOCK : The hell I am. You took the right woman off me, then bound me hand and foot to the wrong one. That's not myth, it's truth. And if you don't like it, you can kneel up, pack your books quietly and go home.

DALEY : Let's get the facts straight first.

LOVELOCK : How is it, you once asked me at the university, that the sexiest girls always come from Star of the Sea convent, Gardenvale? Does the salt air get into their blood? [*Sings.*] "Please don't say no, say maybe . . ." Star of the

Sea girls said yes. Rosemary said yes to me, all through second year philosophy.

DALEY : You've got it all wrong about Rosemary —

LOVELOCK : No I haven't. We walked through Plato together. *The Republic* was the most erotic book in the world for me . . . and then into the republic came the King, the great I am, and it came to pass that the king took the lady away from the commoner and claimed her for his own.

DALEY : I didn't *take* her from you. She *chose* me, of her own free will.

LOVELOCK : It was theft! I couldn't be allowed to get away with a prize like that. What, a dux of the school and an honours man letting silly little Sancho Panza get away with Dulcinea? Heaven forbid. Heaven did forbid. You went behind my back and you won her off me. Never mind that I loved the woman.

DALEY : I loved her too!

LOVELOCK : That didn't give you the right to wreck our relationship.

DALEY : Relationsip? Aren't you building it up a little?

LOVELOCK : Damn it all, we loved each other.

DALEY : She never loved you. Never at any stage.

LOVELOCK : I know why you say that — to make your own action seem less hypocritical.

DALEY : There was no hypocrisy!

LOVELOCK : Yes, hypocrisy. Talking to the Newman Society in public about Christian personalism and the I-thou relationship — and wheedling Rosemary away from me in private. She really believed all that guff about capturing the university for Christ — it was her you wanted to capture, not the university.

DALEY : Honesty? Is that what we're on about? Stripping away the paintwork, is that the caper?

LOVELOCK : Got a needle up your sleeve have you? Going to hit me with a home truth? Come on, what is it? Body odour or bad breath?

DALEY : Rosemary never loved you. She took up with you. She found you amusing. She liked your vulgar, peasant sense of fun. At the time, your kiss-my-royal-Irish-arse cynicism appealed to her.

LOVELOCK : You took her from me, that's one thing. But the time before that you're not having. That is mine. Keep out. Stay on your bloody side of Orrong Road and keep your black hand off it.

DALEY : You're a devil with the myths of others — but you won't let anybody near your own.

LOVELOCK : That year is mine. That year is private property.

DALEY : You got her on the rebound from Collopy, the law student. You were a jester for a disappointed queen. She thought you were a realist, but she was wrong. You're a romantic with one illusion left.

LOVELOCK : And you're here, the thief in the night, to take that too.

DALEY : If I hadn't've won her, somebody else would. The greatest time in your life was a frivolous diversion in hers.

LOVELOCK : She told you.

DALEY : Yes, she told me.

LOVELOCK : And you're telling me for my own good.

DALEY : I'm telling you to stop you looking backwards all the time. Like Brother Dowd used to say, face the front.
[*Pause.*]

LOVELOCK [*subdued, reduced, but still up to an imitation*] : You'll notice we haven't been doing much arithmetic lately. Don't worry, we'll get around to it, we'll get around to it. Brother Dowd, first form, before the onset of Saturday morning classes.

DALEY : It's Saturday morning now, and I'm in no mood for classes.

LOVELOCK : Remember Dowd — [*imitating*] No boy should leave this classroom on a Friday afternoon until he's shaken hands with me — and that, Whiskers Blake, includes you.
[*Daley holds his hand out. Lovelock refuses to shake.*]

LOVELOCK : You took my gang away from me when I was ten, my woman at twenty, and now you've bombed out all I had left. Mission completed. Back you go to base.

DALEY : No absolution?

LOVELOCK : No. Not for what you've done to me. For what you did to her. You won her, then you gave her up for God.

DALEY : That's none of your business.

LOVELOCK [*imitating newsboy*] : "Japanese invade Sydney Harbour." Of course it's my business. She broke me when she left me, then you did the same to her — you broke us both, godammit. You gave up a hell of a lot for God . . . . [*Repenting.*] Sorry, I think I won that unfairly. . . . Fifteen-all, your serve.

DALEY : *You're* the hypocrite. You were *glad* when I gave her up. You were all sympathy on the surface — but your self-satisfaction kept forcing its way out — as if it served her right, for what she'd done to you.

LOVELOCK : Who told you that? Weren't you safe in the seminary?

DALEY : *She* told me that.

LOVELOCK : Then it's a clean ace! I can't even touch the ball! [*Pause*] That's about the lowest thing you could accuse me of . . . and it's true.
[*He wanders about aimlessly.*] The bloody ball's over here somewhere . . . lost in the long grass.

DALEY : Thirty-fifteen then, isn't it. Turn round and face the opposition. You were glad I did it.

LOVELOCK : Glad and sorry, both. Glad you didn't get her. Sorry she had to suffer. . . . No, not sorry. Secretly, it pleased me. I *liked* seeing her suffer.

DALEY [*incredulously*] : You enjoyed seeing the woman you loved suffer!

LOVELOCK : Exactly, you fool. If you love a woman, and she rejects you, the pendulum swings — and there's hate. Love your enemies — and hate those you love! Love, hate, love, hate — twenty-five years later I still carry her round with me in a mental locket — with a split right down the middle of it. The more I retreat from Joy, the more I fall back on — lovely, hateful Rosemary.

DALEY : She's not there any more. She never was.

LOVELOCK : There were moments — passionate moments — bed moments — moments you can't get at.

DALEY : You never went to bed with her, never! You're not remembering the past, you're creating it.

LOVELOCK : She lied to you because she didn't want you to know!

DALEY : Let's test it. Let's see who's right.

LOVELOCK : Test it? What's worrying you — that I got into the garden of delights before you did? What d'you mean test it?

Lie detector? Phone her in the middle of the night — STD to Sydney?

DALEY : She's back in Melbourne with her kids. She's separated.

LOVELOCK : And you've seen her, that's what you're leading up to — come on, that's forty-fifteen — one more cannonball serve and you've got me.

DALEY : She sees *me*. Once a week. After mass.

LOVELOCK : Come on, don't hang round the baseline. Move in for the kill. You're dying to tell me.

[*Pause.*]

Okay, I'll set it up for you. She's alone, she's unhappy, and she wants you back.

DALEY : She hasn't said that!

LOVELOCK : Her weekly visits say it. [*Imitating radio announcer.*] "*Dangerous Corner*, our Lux Radio Theatre production for tonight, is by J.B. Priestley, and stars John Saul and Neva Carr-Glyn." . . . the stage is yours! . . . The tortured priest — bound by a vow of celibacy — and wanting her! Why did Joy bother to go to Wagga when it's all here on her doorstep?

DALEY : I knew you'd cheapen it. That's why I didn't want to tell you.

LOVELOCK : You *loved* telling me. You made it seem as if I dragged it out of you — you couldn't *wait* to tell me. Six-love, six-love to you: my myth's collapsed, and yours is stronger than ever — you've *proved* that God exists! Blind chance couldn't possibly explain how everything comes your way. Always! From the very beginning. Your father rises to lieutenant-colonel without leaving Victoria Barracks. Mine goes to war and gets to corporal.

DALEY : Your father went no further than Exmouth Gulf.

LOVELOCK : That's a damn sight closer to the action than St Kilda Road. All he got for it was a strip of ribbon and a bit of aluminium from Bluey Truscott's crashed plane — yours got two medals and a samurai sword. There's a God all right, and he's divided the world into officers and other ranks. This is the night of the peasants' revolt!

DALEY : I thought you were self-centred, but that's too feeble a word. Your disease is terminal, inoperable. To see what I've just told you as some kind of elaborate plot against yourself, as if everything that happens revolves round you!

LOVELOCK : I'm in the centre of my world, you're in the centre of yours, and now and again our peripheries coincide — I didn't exist for you till the phone rang.

DALEY : I'm asking you to consider my problem as separate from yours — but you're incapable.

LOVELOCK : You're doing what you always do — engulfing me. My problem is now a tinny little echo of yours.

DALEY : I'm not interested in comparing our problems. I'm just saying that if you're trapped, then if it's any consolation, so am I.

LOVELOCK : You're trapped between two desirable alternatives — I inhabit a lower cosmos. I have no choices. My life, if you'll forgive the pretension, is absurd.

DALEY : So's mine. I want God and I want a woman and I can't see why I can't have both.

LOVELOCK : Because, reverend, you took a vow to love him [*pointing upwards*] above all. You're bound to Jehovah like I'm bound to Joy — for good.

DALEY : The toilet! Where's the toilet!

LOVELOCK : That's how it affects me too. Down the hall, first past the frigid bedchamber. Converting it into a coldstore — the temperature in there is zero.... [*Continuing, half to himself, as Daley exits.*] It's not sexual, it's personal. She can't stand me and I can't stand her. I hate her green and yellow Van Goghs, her blue period Picassos, her apron with the giant Cinzano label, her London underground tea towel, her arabica coffee cups, her use of the word fabulous, the tidiness of her house and the sloppiness of her intellect, her restaurant radicalism, her night-school pottery, her futile and desperate attempts to keep up — but she cooks well, I'll give her that, she's a darned good cook.... [*Still calling after him.*] Know why I used to hate inviting kids to play at my place in the old days? Because of the toilet. We had a plain ordinary house, but something went wrong with the plans when they got to the lavatory — [*Imitating, American accent.*] "This is Ripley's believe-it-or-not. Stories of all that's weird and wonderful in this wide wide world. Eleven-year-old Master J. Lovelock, of East St Kilda, Melbourne, has the smallest toilet in the world. The door is right against your knees. You have to wipe yourself sitting down. And when you bend to pull up your trousers, you bump your head." [*He mimes a little of this, falls to carpet, crawls to stereo, puts on an old Andrews Sisters record. Enter Daley.*]

DALEY : The Andrews Sisters.

LOVELOCK : Picked it up at a church bazaar. Remember your joke about 'em, confided to me behind your hand in Anglin's French class — "Hey Lovelock — what's got six tits and sings? The Andrews Sisters!" Patti, Maxene, and Laverne!

DALEY [*sings*] : "That crazy thing, the chicka-chicka-boom-chick ... chick-chicka-chicka-boom, chick-chicka-chicka-boom." There was one sexy one, one plain one, and one sort of in between —

LOVELOCK : Patti was the sexy one —

DALEY : Maxene was —

LOVELOCK : Don't change the subject! To hell with the Andrews Sisters! I want to talk about Rosemary — maybe she's gone to fat, fat and grey with calves like chianti bottles —

DALEY : I hate to disappoint you — she's forty-two, she's got four kids, she's more beautiful than ever — and every Sunday she comes a little closer.... There's been a number of theories about why you rang *me* but none so far about why I happened to come over. I seized on your phone call, couldn't get over here quick enough — because this weekend she's on her own — no kids, no in-laws — just her, waiting.

LOVELOCK : For you.

DALEY : Yes, for me. I was hoping you'd see me through the night. So far you've been no help at all. It's so long since you've experienced the emotion you've forgotten what it's like.

LOVELOCK : Don't misunderstand me. I haven't spent the last twenty years pining for Rosemary. But adultery's a privilege that only comes with marriage — not holy orders.

DALEY : You can't bear the thought of us together. Don't dress it up as moral advice.

LOVELOCK : No, I can't bear the thought of it — but that's irrelevant. I'm thinking of *your* problem. Cut and run, that's what you told me to do. Get a transfer. A lonely little parish in the Mallee.

DALEY : I can't run, I've run out of wind. I'm drifting.

LOVELOCK : No one just drifts. You have to will yourself to drift, and that means giving in. If you're too tired to move stay put. Tread water. Lie low. Wait for it to pass. Immobility is wisdom. Stay in Melchisedech's royal house — it's dangerous to leave the palace.

DALEY : Immobility is wisdom! Inertia is strength! Never in the whole time I've known you have you actually done anything. All you've done is sat down the back of the class and sniggered. You put a dead bat up to life whenever it comes near you.

LOVELOCK : Exactly. And now you may go [*holding out hand*]. You have my permission to leave the room.

DALEY : You go! Leave your dull little lady, your dull little job.

LOVELOCK [*sings*] : "Bongo Bongo Bongo, I don't wanna leave the Congo, oh no no no no no —" You're the shepherd, I'm only the merino — *you* make the move.

DALEY : I'll *move!* I'll show you what to do!

[*Picks up phone.*]

LOVELOCK [*pulling phone plug from wall*] : "Bosco, I am saved!" Caption in silent movie on St John Bosco in parish hall, May 1941. Correct me if I'm wrong, but did we not also see on that same chilly afternoon a newsreel on the resistance fighters in Belgium? — "Belgian girls of sixteen or seventeen were used as playthings by German officers."

DALEY : If I don't act I'll end up infested by borers like you.

LOVELOCK : I'm the one who's supposed to be committing suicide, not you. Say a Hail Mary and wait for the temptation to go away.

DALEY : It won't go away.

LOVELOCK : Then go away from it.

DALEY : If there's any going away — we'll do it together.

LOVELOCK : You can't break out of a priesthood and into a marriage. You can't crash through two walls. You'll be pulp, you'll have chips all over your shoulders. . . . *I'll* ring her up and tell her Don Quixote is unavailable — but fat old Sancho's still waiting on his faithful ass.

DALEY : You *won't* ring her — and neither will I. Not tonight or any other. You're afraid to leave your house and I'm afraid to leave mine.

LOVELOCK [*reciting*] : "Cold blows the winter wind over hill and heather. Thick drives the rain and my roof is dust." [*Imitating*] Don't make it sing-song. Keep those vowels rolling. A boy that can speak well can hold his head up anywhere. —[*Resumes normal voice*] One o'clock and all's well. Time you went home.

DALEY : Home? Where's home?

LOVELOCK : You've got Brighton and I've got Blackburn and that's where we stay — on our selections.

DALEY : Dry Mallee scrubland.

LOVELOCK : And the last thing our great-grandparents did was walk off their blocks. You stay put and wait for the harvest — that's the Edict of Nantes.

DALEY : And the Diet of Worms. The rain never comes. Never!

LOVELOCK : Look down, not up then — into the ice-cream of memory! It's all waiting for you down there at the bottom of the canister, frozen, the pure white vanilla. That's where home is. Home's the Palais front stalls as the lights are going down. We've been waiting all week for this — *Buck Privates!* Abbott and Costello have joined the army by mistake — and Lou's about to step into the ring to fight a soldier built like a gorilla. Wham! Lou gets knocked to the ground — but why's the referee counting in twos? "What happened to one, three, five, seven, nine?" says Lou. "They're odd, those numbers," the ref says, "I don't like 'em." "Put 'em in!" yells Lou from the mat. "I like 'em!" End of round one. Bud Abbott, coaching Lou in the white corner: "Now when you get back in there give him the old one-three, see? The one-three." Lou— "Wait on, what happened to two?" "Ah," says Bud, "two *you* get!" [*He mimes some of this, finally falling to floor, where, at the end of the joke, he starts swimming*]

DALEY : Are you boxing or are you swimming?

LOVELOCK : Daley and Lovelock in the fifty yards at the school swimming sports at the Richmond baths.

DALEY : — and you failing to finish.

LOVELOCK [*swimming his way over to stereo*] : I'm finishing . . . I'm finishing with Rosemary — her favourite record in 1952 — the end! The goal! The destination!

DALEY : I don't want to hear her favourite record!

LOVELOCK [*putting disc on turntable*] : But you know what it is!

DALEY : A Little Night Music!

[*By now he's collected his things and is on his way to the door, when the music catches him, stops him.*]

LOVELOCK [*his voice audible over the music which should be soft at first, then louder*] : Together we face it — and then you go home!

[*They both stand listening. Lights slowly down.*]

Eugene Flockhart's Desk

A Radio Play

CHARACTERS

FLOCKHART : a middle-aged public servant
MULLALY : a young public servant
OXENBURGH : a public servant
SMITHSON : a callow messenger boy
TREVASKIS : a public servant
MACNIFF : a public servant
DOLORES : a typist
HUNTER : Flockhart's boss
PRESNELL : a public servant

Sounds of a large door opening, then swinging back and forth as it closes. Footfalls approach us along a vinyl corridor: FLOCKHART *is arriving for work.*

VOICE 1 : Morning Flockhart.
FLOCKHART [*obviously preoccupied, withdrawn*]: M? Eh? Oh, morning, morning.
[*More footfalls.*]
VOICE 2 [*cheery*] : Good morning Mr Flockhart.
FLOCKHART [*irritable*]: Yes, yes, morning, morning ... [*To himself.*] What's good about it?
VOICE 3 : Too good to be inside.
FLOCKHART : Yes, yes, too true ... [*To himself.*] Pointless exchange of banalities ... if I can just get to my office without another obscene courtesy ... the next clerk that says good morning gets a whack across the head with my paper ... hurry, hurry, nearly there ... [*Door opening and closing.*] Ha! Safe! My little cage at last! God, what an ordeal, running the gauntlet over the vinyl tiles ... say good morning to you one minute and assassinate you in a memo the next ... [*Sigh of relief.*] — ha! [*He breathes deep.*] Morning files. Goodday gliderclips. *Bonjour* desk. Salutations telephone. And all hail, oh mighty Minister up on the wall! ... [*Quieter.*] That hideous visage looking down at me, that framed portrait in plasticine, watching, watching ... I'm leaving you today Minister ... I'm going to miss you Minister ... what a strange expression you have on your face ... like a goanna emerging from a hole in a tree trunk ... at once menacing and bewildered ... my god, I

must be going mad! Eight forty-three! Two minutes early!
One hundred and twenty seconds all to myself... let's see
what's in the paper... "Answers From The Oracle: If the
bottom bill of your cockatoo is twisted, correcting it by surgery could be both difficult and expensive. The Oracle suggests you visit the zoo and ask the attendants the question
that worries you. As the zoo has a lot of expensive and rare
birds, they would know what to do in the circum-
stances"... good Lord... hey, wait on, get this: "Mouth-to-
beak Resuscitation Effort Saves Rooster" — interesting,
interesting — I'll have that for my poultry file... [*Makes
rooster noise.*] cock-a-doodle-doo... stop that Flockhart,
stop it... scissors, scissors... [*Making hen-like noises.*]
buk-buk-buk-buk- take a hold of yourself man, control
yourself — buk-buk-buk- stop that!
[*A knock.*]
Whassat? Buk-buk-buk-buk- [*Clears throat, readies himself for normality.*]
Come in, come in.

MULLALY : Mister Flockhard?

FLOCKHART : Buk-buk-wha? Flockhart my boy, hart, Old Flock's
not hard. Flock's soft, soft, like feathers... buk-buk-buk-
stop that, stop it...

MULLALY : I'm Jack Mullaly. Mr Hunter told me to see you.

FLOCKHART : Ah, the new man! Welcome to the service Mr
Mullaly. Welcome to Room 41. They call it Siberia, and
I've spent the last fourteen years here. When Mr Hunter,
my former colleague, was promoted over my head, he made
it his business to have me shifted to this room.

MULLALY : Is Canberra always as cold as this? I'm freezing.

FLOCKHART : Canberra? Always cold. Even on the hottest days of
summer. Either you're accepted and you suffocate, or
you're out, and you freeze to death... you must make it
your business to get out of Room 41 as soon as possible. A
Rip Van Winkle of a room. When you finally leave it, you'll
blink in the sunshine like a startled rabbit... unpack your
things and make yourself comfortable... Hunker down for
the winter... preen and ruffle your feathers, tuck your
head under your wing, and... buk-buk-buk... stop that,
stop it.

MULLALY [*half to himself*]: Pen ... paper ... pins and clips ...
  rubber bands ... date stamp, blotter ...
FLOCKHART : Are you mad Mullaly? Bringing in your own stationery? Don't you realize these things are provided in the public service? In fact that *are* the public service.
MULLALY : I thought it was better to come prepared, that's all.
FLOCKHART : Prepared Mr Mullaly? Prepared? That's a strange
  word. For what, may I ask? For what?
MULLALY : For work, that's what. It might sound a little unusual
  in Canberra, but I like to be occupied — to be doing something.
FLOCKHART : Don't we all my boy, don't we all. But not everyone
  is so fortunate. No doubt a bit of "work" as you call it will
  come your way one of these days ... in its own good time ...
  [*Musing, slightly incredulous still.*] Work eh? Hmm ...
  work ... buk-buk-buk- stop that.
MULLALY : Is there something I could do right now? Or do I sit
  here twiddling my thumbs to prevent frostbite?
FLOCKHART : Patience, patience. Mr Hunter will no doubt assign
  you something when he sees his way clear. You'll get an
  industry to investigate. A little sector you can call your
  own. Mine is the poultry industry. Just finished an exhaus-
  tive report on the subject: "The Australian Poultry Industry: A Diagnosis". A catchy title is it not? There are ail-
  ments in the industry and these are tellingly pinpointed. A
  few heads will roll on the chopping block — buk-buk-buk-
  aaark! — stop that — but not mine. I'll be safe, gone, flown
  the nest — flap-flap — you follow me?
MULLALY : You're leaving? I didn't know that.
FLOCKHART : Yes. I go this very day. I was given a *choice* — either
  retire on account of my weak heart, or transfer to Management Services — an insult, to say the least. So, I'm — retiring.
MULLALY : I'm sorry to hear that — just as we're getting acquain-
  ted —
FLOCKHART : — And very soon you'll take my place: Research
  Officer, Grade Eight, Room 41, Bureau of Statistical Infor-
  mation, Commerce Division, sounds good, does it not?
MULLALY : Most impressive. I think I'll smoke to that. Cigarette?
FLOCKHART : Not at this moment. I eat two apples, walk three

miles, and smoke four cigarettes a day. The first at morning tea time.

MULLALY : I could do with some tea . . . A cup of tea, a Scotch Finger, and thou . . .

FLOCKHART : The tea trolley! Wait'll you see it! Hissing and fuming like Stephenson's Rocket. The inmates emerge from their cubicles, stained tea cups in hand — and Madge does the honours. The liquid looks not unlike the River Murrumbidgee at flood time, detritus included. A few pleasantries are exchanged, then back they go to their cells, clutching their solitary biscuit —

MULLALY : *One* biscuit? Only one biscuit?

FLOCKHART : One biscuit. A memo came round only last week — it's a document I treasure . . . hang on, here it is, get this — "To all staff. It has come to my notice that privileges are being abused during the tea intervals. It is alleged" — cagey, cagey — "that some officers are apportioning to themselves" — wonderful! Magnificent! — "two, or even three biscuits, so that by the time the trolley reaches the upper floors, none is left. In order that equitable distribution be achieved" — superb, superb — "officers are hereby instructed to take one biscuit only with their beverage" — signed A.E. Simmons, Amenities Officer.

MULLALY : Amenities Officer? Surely that's not his full time job?

FLOCKHART : Not only that — he has a staff of two. A girl to do his stencilling, and a surly youth with a tendency to acne — [*Phone rings.*] — Damn that phone, never stops — Information — what is it you want? Just a moment . . . [*Flicking of pages.*] . . . damn fools — buk-buk-buk- stop that — according to the *Government Gazette*, the Tariff Board is currently considering the following items — rubberized undergarments, wheel-mounted hospital stretchers, and unrendered goat's fat. I thank you. [*Phone down.*]

MULLALY : The Amenities Officer has a staff of two — to look after the biscuits?

FLOCKHART : Oh no — there's the ping pong equipment, the toilet rolls, the organizing of get-togethers, picture nights, cricket matches — you'll join the Staff Club, of course —

MULLALY : I'd like to get to know some of the staff first, if you don't mind. Working with people is one thing. Mixing with them socially — well, that's another matter.

FLOCKHART : I don't mind my friend — but they will. You'll join — or else. You'll go on their alpine weekends to Thredbo — or else. [*Imitating German accent.*] — Ve haff ways of making you enjoy yourself — here, here, mind those papers!

MULLALY : Reports, endless reports — my desk drawers are stuffed with them! "Opportunities For Growth In The Hog Lard Sector" . . . "Tung Nut Oil Prospects 1949" . . . I don't want any of this!

FLOCKHART : Careful, careful. Never destroy a file or report. Regard them as Hindus do animal life . . . [*Phone rings.*] . . . damned phone. Yes? Oh, Mr Hunter . . . [*with irony.*] . . . and good morning to you . . . yes, I'll tell him . . . a farewell presentation for me this afternoon? How kind, how kind . . . *au revoir.* [*Phone down.*] Good news Mr Mullaly. Your career has begun in earnest. Mr Hunter would like you to commence research into the domestic hardware industry . . . potato peelers, eggbeaters, whisks, swizzle sticks — a fascinating field.

MULLALY : A typewriter — that's what I need. A typewriter. And then — into it!

FLOCKHART : Stationery supplies may be requisitioned from the appropriate officer only after three each afternoon. Stationery Officer. Never has Mr Oxenburgh been better described. Oxenburgh rules his domain of quarto and foolscap like Caligula — [*Knock on door.*] — come in — speaking of Roman emperors — good morning Oxenburgh.

OXENBURGH : Morning. Up in the mountains knee-deep in a trout-stream, that's where I'd like to be.

MULLALY [*whispering*]: Those ears? Why's he wearing those extraordinary ears?

FLOCKHART : Ssh . . . later, later.

OXENBURGH : Excuse me Flockhart — if I could just have a quick dip into your drawers —

FLOCKHART : My drawers? What the devil are you on about man?

OXENBURGH : I'm taking an inventory, that's what I'm on about. Sorting out which are your possessions and which are ours. Regular procedure when an officer is leaving — I thought you'd know that.

FLOCKHART : Ours? Which possessions are ours? You feel one of a team do you Oxenburgh? Part of a cosy family?

OXENBURGH [*ignoring him*]: One blotter pad, large . . . ballpoint pens, four . . . one ruler, featuring Australian native timbers . . . one miniature Australian flag on a silver standard . . .

FLOCKHART : Mullaly, there are nearly a million public servants in this country, and when they line up in their dark suits and say *ours* all together, the noise is like a thunderclap.

OXENBURGH [*oblivious*] : One piece of carpet, grey . . . one hat and coat rack, antique . . . one sub-executive desk, three-drawer — [*sound of drawer opening.*] — containing — this is a disgrace, the smell in this drawer is appalling — one rotting orange, two crusts, four apple cores, crumbs, glider clips, rubber bands, Aspro packet, one gas bill unpaid — like a damned fowlpen in there.

MULLALY : Excuse me — Mr Oxenburgh —

OXENBURGH : You're new aren't you?

MULLALY : Yes, I'm new. The name's Mullaly. Started this morning —

OXENBURGH : Two Band-aids, unused — one snapshot of a young woman, faded — several newspaper cuttings, yellowed —

MULLALY [*pressing on*]: — I was wondering if I could get hold of a typewriter — to start my research.

OXENBURGH : — one paperback entitled *The Gulag Archipelago* — one packet of Quik-Eze — won't a biro do?

MULLALY : — to do my work properly I'm afraid I'm going to need a typewriter.

OXENBURGH : — three postage stamps, one aerogramme, four yellow tablets, loose — it's irregular Mr Mullaly, highly irregular — let's go and have a look — kindly leave the desk as you once found it Flockhart — otherwise I'll have to call in the fumigators.

FLOCKHART : Certainly Oxenburgh — what a pity I removed my pornographic photos only yesterday — off you both go now.

OXENBURGH : I'll see you later Flockhart. At the farewell. Personally, I can't wait for it. Never has a retirement been so eagerly awaited. The whole department's looking forward to it . . . follow me Mullaly . . . it'll be the greatest blessing this place has had since air-conditioning.[*Slams door.*]

FLOCKHART[*yelling after him*] : Cipher! Squirrel! Sycophant! . . .
[*Sighs.*] peace at last . . . ah . . . buk-buk-buk- [*Knock on door.*] come in. Oh it's you Smithson . . . are you wearing socks my lad? You are? Then you're going to have to pull them up, pull 'em up. Three days ago I left an important memo in my out tray addressed to Mr Hunter, who lives a mere twenty yards away. It has not yet reached its destination.

SMITHSON : Sorry sir. What did it look like exactly?

FLOCKHART : A white piece of paper Smithson, foolscap size, bearing typed information. A not uncommon sight in this building. There'd be roughly, at any given moment, one million such items on the premises.

SMITHSON : I'll do what I can sir — here's something for you in the meantime — just in from America.

FLOCKHART : Thank you my boy, thank you, I've been waiting for this. *Doctor Magnusson's Turkey Diseases Manual.* Does it, or does it not, verify the findings in section five of my poultry monograph? — wait for it, wait for it — ah yes, very good — excellent Smithson, excellent. Consider your socks pulled up Smithson.

SMITHSON : Thanks sir.
[*Door opens.*]

MULLALY [*entering*]: Look at this. It's huge, it's ancient, but — [*putting it down with an effort and tapping a few keys.*] — it works! — tap-tap-tap- it works eh! — tap-tap-tap.

FLOCKHART : Quiet! Never mind about that — listen man, listen!

MULLALY : I don't hear anything — listen to what?

FLOCKHART : After a while you develop trained ears, like a bat . . . hear it? The sweet distant song of the tea trolley . . . ahah! It comes! All round the barnyard, the farm animals are emerging . . . now for the clack of cups, the breaking of biscuits, and the symposium of meteorology . . . ahah . . . [*Going.*] . . . excuse me . . . buk-buk-buk-birrrk-buk-buk-buk- chickenfeed!

MULLALY [*indifferent, tapping on*]: The quick brown fox jumps over the lazy dog . . . hmm . . . seems okay . . . must have been one of the very first models invented by the look of it — [*Phone rings.*] — Yes? This is Mullaly. The what? The time book? — I didn't sign? — I'm sorry, I'm new here, you see . . . yes — yes — I'll tell him. Good morning. [*Phone down.*]

FLOCKHART [*entering*]: Aha . . . look at it . . . I think she takes it straight from the lower reaches of the River Molonglo . . . silt, yabbies, cats' corpses and all . . . [*Sipping.*] hmm . . . grey and stewed. As if a possum has been boiled in with the water. None for you?

MULLALY : On second thoughts, no, thanks all the same . . . that was Mr Trevaskis of Personnel. I didn't sign the time book. But he'll overlook it till this evening . . . He's coming up here now — to see you. By the way — Oxenburgh. Those ears. He had false ears. Has he had plastic surgery?

FLOCKHART : Of a kind, yes. The Regulations state that on certain occasions, such as the day someone is leaving, the super-annuant's colleagues are required to don ceremonial regalia.

MULLALY : Good lord — ears?

FLOCKHART : See up there on the wall? The hideous mask-like fea-tures of the Minister of our Department. Officers may wear certain parts of that visage according to seniority. Oxenburgh has done ten years' hard labour — that entitles him to the ears.

MULLALY : How quaint. And fifteen years?

FLOCKHART : The ears and nose.

MULLALY : And twenty?

FLOCKHART : After twenty years, you may wear the dreadful mask in its entirety. The further you advance, the closer you get to the Minister. [*Knock.*] Aha! — Prepare for the nose and ears of — [*Door opens.*] — Trevaskis! Good morning!

TREVASKIS : Good morning? When all the clocks in the building are two minutes slow? And fifteen people rolled in after eight forty-five? And I have to go round wearing this — paraphernalia — just because you've finally come to your senses and decided to leave?

FLOCKHART : Your own nose looked impressive enough — but with the Minister's sacred proboscis on top of it — the effect is superb! A cockatoo! Here cocky . . . scratch cocky . . . buk-buk-buk.

TREVASKIS : I'm scratching you alright Flockhart — right off the time book for good . . . Mr Mullaly, you'll be signing book two on counter four. On at eight forty-five, off at six minutes past five — on the dot.

FLOCKHART : Because at precisely eight forty-six, Mr Trevaskis begins his dawn patrol, ruling his red lines under the last names in the books. Then on his way back he pauses to inspect his snares, seeing who he's caught in his little wires.

TREVASKIS : By the way Flockhart — your latecomings over the past month happen to total two hours thirty minutes —

FLOCKHART : — listen Mullaly, listen — if one's unpunctuality exceeds thirty minutes per month — explain it to him Oh Nose and Ears, explain —

TREVASKIS : Your emolument is reduced accordingly.

FLOCKHART : No eventuality is unprovided for, you see — even if you should expire on the premises, there is a procedure.

TREVASKIS : — so that your final stipend, Flockhart, will be reduced by $20. Good morning.[*Door opens, closes.*]

FLOCKHART [*yelling after him*]: Petty despot! . . . [*To himself.*] Lording it over their tiny principalities, their sharp little tails up ready to sting the moment you touch them . . . well I'm touching them today . . . I've a few scores to settle . . . buk-buk-buk . . .

MULLALY [*ignoring him*]: "The Domestic Hardware Industry: An Investigation" — there. How does it sound?

FLOCKHART [*claps*]: Magnificent. Best seller on both sides of the Atlantic. Book-of-the-Month selection. I can see it up on the screen, in Vistavision — the clash of vegetable graters in stereophonic sound.

MULLALY [*talks to himself while typing*]: The domestic hardware industry . . . is noteable for . . .

FLOCKHART : Yes, tap away. I started like you, full of enthusiasm and fire — and what have I got for it — one set of the Minister's ears and nose, as new, immaculate condition, one owner and totally unsaleable . . . better do some filing I suppose . . . funny word, filing . . . prisoners to it do iron bars to try to escape . . . oh damn and blast — I've torn my trouser cuff on the edge of that drawer — what fool left it wide open like that? Wait, I know, I'll claim compensation for it — if the drawer was left open, it's negligence on my part — but if [*Closing it.*] it was closed, then the Commonwealth is liable — [*Picking up phone, dialling.*] —

that you MacNiff? How is the gout? Better I trust? Mr MacNiff, a strange thing happened to me on my way to my desk this morning — would you mind? I thank you.[*Phone down.*] Mr Mullaly — Mr Mullaly — if you stop that infernal tapping for a moment, I am going to give you an exclusive peep into the tiny, whirring sprockets of the departmental mind.

MULLLALY : Look I really must get on with this. The domestic hardware industry is an enormous field, absolutely vast —

FLOCKHART : Never mind about that, you've got years, years — but do I hear the heavy tread of MacNiff — let us do battle with him, match wits — [*Knock.*] — come in — [*Door opens.*] — welcome MacNiff, welcome—

MACNIFF : Is it important Flockhart — I'm very busy, really I am — everybody seems to be claiming compensation for something.

FLOCKHART : I've been busy too my friend. That's why I'd like you to take a long hard look at this trouser cuff. What do you see?

MACNIFF : Torn Flockhart. Torn. Anyone can see that.

FLOCKHART : Just so MacNiff. Torn. Indubitably. And how? A freakish accident. I caught it — on that cabinet drawer — on the handle — in the course of my duties —

MACNIFF : Caught it on the *corner* of the drawer by the look of it — when it was open, I'll wager — open when it should be closed.

FLOCKHART : Oho no — it *was* closed. No negligence on my part. It was closed, as it should be when not in use — and I caught my cuff on the handle.

MACNIFF : That handle's curved Flockhart — you couldn't have torn it on the handle.

FLOCKHART : *You* might call it curved MacNiff — I call it — squarish — with perhaps a fraction of smoothing to round it off.

MACNIFF : Oh come on — how could a cuff — how could a cuff—

FLOCKHART : It's smooth, but not smooth enough to prevent an officer being impaled upon it while innocently going about his duties. Mr Mullaly — would you call this a rounded or a square edge?

MULLALY   [*who's been intermittently tapping during this exchange, in a way that suggests that, though he'd like to get on with his work, he's fascinated by the case's triviality*]: I'm sorry, I've got work to do — research — investigation —

FLOCKHART : Your opinion, Mullaly, on a point of fact.

MULLALY : The handle's — rounded. A rounded edge, surely.

MACNIFF : I thank you. As a result, Flockhart, I'm afraid I cannot see my way clear to consider the question of compensation.

FLOCKHART : — can't see your way clear? Are you in need of optical attention?

MACNIFF : Thank you Flockhart. I don't fancy being insulted in the discharge of my duties.

FLOCKHART : Discharge of your duties? Are you losing blood man? I didn't know you had any.

MACNIFF : I've got blood all right — and it's close to boiling point — I'd like to wring your scrawny rooster neck.

FLOCKHART : Don't lay a hand on me my friend — I'd break your arm and you'd break a regulation — good afternoon.

[*Slams door as* MACNIFF *exits.*]
Well Mullaly, that was excellent — you turned king's evidence against me, and I lost my claim for compensation.

MULLALY : Look here — those handles *are* rounded, and that's all there is to it. All right? No more about it.

FLOCKHART : Keep it up, keep it up. Toe the line — you'll be an eight-seven-two before you know where you are.

MULLALY : And what the hell is an eight-seven-two when it's at home? Isn't there anything straightforward in this damned place?

FLOCKHART : An eight-seven-two denotes a grade, a salary. Six-two-four, seven-one-six, eight-seven-two — it's a code you'll master pretty soon. It's one of the beauties of the service — your status can be computed with mathematical accuracy — your salary's known, your address is known, your behaviour is known — you'll be hard put to it to sin in Canberra, Mullaly, believe me.

MULLALY [*tapping*]: I'd like to get on with my work.

FLOCKHART : Work? Work? You wouldn't even know where to start. [*Phone rings.*] Siberia? Yes? What? There's a damned printing press in my room, that's why I can't hear you my friend. What items? Just a second. [*Flipping of pages.*] Yes, there is a quota for artificial flowers in the Cameroons — but opportunities are wide open for rubber goods in the Upper Volta. And good day to *you* sir. [*Tapping proceeds.*] Just a minute, just a minute. There's a procedure for an industrial investigation Mullaly, and it goes something like this — [*He sings or chants ritualistically.*] One — consult all relevant papers in the library. Two — obtain names and addresses of all manufacturers. Three —

MULLALY : Listen, I know how to conduct an investigation. I'll go my own way thanks very much.

FLOCKHART : Oh, you will, will you? Very well then — you go straight ahead — you'll learn soon enough — [*Timid knocking.*] — oh, but look who's here — it's Dolores — knocking at the door of my heart — [*Bursts into song again.*] — "A Sleepy Lagoon, a Tropical Moon, and You . . . " Mullaly, meet Dolores, the princess of the pink files, my beautiful little chickadee — buk-buk-buk-

DOLORES [*awkward, yet coquettish*] : Hello — it's so cold in here — it's always cold in here.

MULLALY : The pink files? How many damned colours are there?

DOLORES : There's a funny one in this lot Mr Flockhart —

FLOCKHART : The pinks are copies of all outgoing correspondence Mullaly. The diligent officer scans them all. I just get Dolores to read me out any funny ones. The rest I ignore — pure toilet paper.

DOLORES : Listen to this one. [*Reading.*] "The Manager, Outback Stuffed Kangaroo Company, Parramatta Road, Sydney: Dear Sir or Madam. With reference to your proposal to export toy wallabies with music box in pouch that plays Waltzing Matilda — [*Furious tapping.*] — when the forepaw is agitated" —

FLOCKHART : Do you mind? I can't hear Dolores —

MULLALY : I'm sorry, I've got work to do.

DOLORES : I'd better go Mr Flockhart. Miss Hepburn's in one of her moods — if I spend too much time talking with the men I get the sharp edge of her tongue.

FLOCKHART : I know, I know — that snappy old tartar will take a bite out of your ankle soon as look at you. You'll have teethmarks in your calf before long Mullaly — no one escapes Miss Hepburn, the crusty old carp of the typing pool ... give us a peck then before you go Dolores — come on, a peck — buk-buk-buk.

DOLORES : Oh Mr Flockhart—

FLOCKHART : Come on, it's my last day. Please. A peck, a peck ...
[*They kiss.*]

DOLORES : That was more than a peck — Mr Flockhart, I'm surprised at you — a man your age.

FLOCKHART : Goodbye you beautiful caged bird you — goodbye my chicken — buk-buk-

DOLORES : 'Bye Mr Flockhart— I'd better fly —
[*Door closes.*]

FLOCKHART : Fly away my Dolores — can't you just see her — her wings spread — my blue bird of happiness — gliding down, down to the shady waters of the typing pool — buk-buk-buk- stop that.

MULLALY : Will you stop that buk-buking! I've had enough. It's like a damned chicken coop in here.

FLOCKHART : You go tap-tap all day — why can't I go buk-buk?

MULLALY : If lunch time doesn't come soon —

FLOCKHART : Saved my boy, saved! Only five minutes to go! How do I know? They're starting to trot down to our toilet. First there'll be Morris from Accounts — he'll sit with the morning paper over his knees, emitting noises like the mating call of the sea-cow. Then comes little Shanahan from Management Services. He'll roll off about a hundred feet of toilet paper, put it in his pocket, and take it home to his wife and six kids —

MULLALY : Enough! I've had enough! Got to get out!
[*Door bangs shut.*]

FLOCKHART [*breathing sigh of relief*]: And goodbye to you sir ...
[*Hums to himself, obviously happy to be alone.*] ...
[*Sings.*] *Une Poule Sur Un Mur — Qui Pecorait Du Pain Dur* ... a sip of lunch, a bit of a read, and a snooze ... [*Pop of cork, as from flask.*] ... that's what I'm going to miss, these snoozes ... [*Reads.*] "The Australian Poultry Industry, in its untidy sprawl and ramshackle organization, may not unreasonably be likened to a barnyard" ... what an opening Flockhart, what an opening — that'll make 'em sit up on their perches — buk-buk-buk- enough, enough of

that — and your conclusion Flockhart, I love this bit —
[*Reads.*] "Just as certain operators remove the beaks of
these helpless creatures to prevent cannibalism in the cages,
some similar action might be necessary against the per-
petrators themselves, in order to protect the luckless con-
sumer from the sharpness of their practices"... that'll
cause a few flutters in the dovecotes — no wonder they
want me to go... one more sip [*Cork pops.*] and let's put
the feet up... [*Breathes deep, then quiet snores...*]

VOICES [*whispering, dreamlike*]: Flock-hart! Flock-hart!
Foolhart! Hartfool! Chickenhart! Hencoop! Flockfool!
Hartburn! Mad, mad, mad! Flock off, wheathart! Nutty old
bachelor! Bye bye Lonelyhart!... [*More snores.*]...
Who's that, pushing the tea trolley? — good god! It's
Flockhart — he's the new Minister! He's been promoted —
to Minister!

[*Flourish of trumpets.*]

FLOCKHART : Down on your knees, all of you! Present your petitions, quickly!

FIRST PETITIONER : Your eminence, your eminence! My office is so
crowded. I have never destroyed a file, not one! They fill my
cupboards, my drawers, they block the light from my window —

FLOCKHART : Enough! Knock down a wall, take some of the space
from the adjoining staff room, and requisition for a smaller
table tennis table. Next!

SECOND PETITIONER : Oh emperor of the world and the galaxies,
hear me! This very day Mr Trevaskis ruled the red line on
the time book two minutes early, making me appear
unpunctual —

FLOCKHART : Stand up Trevaskis!

TREVASKIS : Have mercy oh lord! Spare me, oh sultan of the
cosmos!

FLOCKHART : Silence! In future you will approach the time books
at snail's pace on all fours, and rule the red line at the base
of each page.

VOICE : What wisdom! Another Solomon!

FLOCKHART : Quick, quick, one more only — you, you.

THIRD PETITIONER : When the paymaster comes, oh divinely-appointed one, they ring a small bell — unfortunately I am unable to hear its tinkle from my room —

FLOCKHART : Have the bell replaced by a large gong, mounted on the tea trolley — [*Snaps his fingers.*] — at once, at once — and when the paymaster comes, let it be beaten thus — [*Bangs gong two or three times.*]

VOICE : More oh master!

FLOCKHART : Enough! Give them rubber toffee apples to ease the pain in their gums — to the typing pool, quickly!
[*Sounds of typing.*]
Girls! Girls! I have good news! I, Flockhart, have been made, by the grace of god, Minister!
[*Teeny-bopper shrieks and sighs of approval.*]
Turn on the music! Uncork the bottles! Away with your Dear Sirs or Madams! Today we go mad!
[*Loud music, mixed in, if possible, with hen-and-rooster noises and the flapping of wings.*]
Girls! Girls! There's room for you all in my heart —
[*Music and sounds fade.*]

MULLALY : Flockhart! Flockhart! You alright?

FLOCKHART : Lies! Lies I say! Girls! Wait! What? Of course I'm alright.

MULLALY : You were talking in your sleep, and waving your arms up and down as if you were flying.

FLOCKHART : I was having a flocknight — I mean a nightmare. Can't people even *dream* in privacy these days? . . . I hate lunchtime. Lowest part of the day. Something to do with the bodily metabolism apparently. Some go to the hotel, some play table tennis, and others just sit over their lunches with this awful feeling in the pits of their stomachs. I ease the pain by going to sleep.

MULLALY : I've heard enough about your pain. And you know what I think? It's self-inflicted. You're doing it to yourself.

FLOCKHART : Ah no my boy, it's real. The Canberra pain. Get out while you've got the chance. Go back to Melbourne. Once you're settled, they've got you trapped — in your little brick house with the lawns to mow and the car to polish — you've got nowhere to escape — you can't hide in the windy spaces of the planned city!

MULLALY : I can't go back now for heaven's sake — I've only just
arrived!

FLOCKHART [*not listening*]: A city, that's what I dream of.
Exhaust fumes, neon lights, used car lots — vulgar, noisy —
but alive! Forest Lawn — you know that burial place in
California? — all nicely laid out, grass, parks, curving ways
— that's Canberra! A Forest Lawn with vertical corpses!
Get out! Run! Flee the necropolis!
[*Phone rings.*]
Hello? You want what? The situation with black plastic
toilet seats in Pakistan? — just a moment, just a moment —
[*Half to himself.*] get out . . . flee . . . quickly, while there's
time . . . spread the wings and fly . . . the quota situation is
not good for toilet seats — the entire cabinet is coming
down hard on them at the moment — what? And bully to
you too sir.
[*Bangs phone down.*]
[MULLALY *taps away and whistles, while* FLOCKHART
*continues to mutter to himself. Suddenly he snaps out of
it.*]

FLOCKHART : Wait, wait a minute. That tune you're whistling —
"The Girl With The Flaxen Hair"!

MULLALY : That's right. I like Debussy. How about this?
[*Whistles* "Clair de Lune".]

FLOCKHART : Never mind about that. Whistle "The Girl With The
Flaxen Hair" again. Quickly!
[MULLALY *obliges.*]
. . . Of all the music in the repertoire, you have to choose
that . . . Some years ago, I had an — involvement. A young
woman in Accounts. I used to get to the office early — for
the sheer pleasure of seeing her arrive. She was tall, majes-
tic — I'd stand at the window and watch her, and that tune
of Debussy's would go round and round in my head . . .
[MULLALY *taps away, not really listening, and whistles the
tune quietly as* FLOCKHART *proceeds, largely to himself.*]
For months I watched her. This building — this great
dreary catacomb — became a place of hidden delights. Life
is cruel Mullaly, life is run on Ivan the Terrible lines — but
every so often even he wearied of his cruelty and indulged
some pathetic subject. So it was with me. It was at the office

party one Christmas Eve. I was helping myself to a sandwich, when I sensed this sun, this glow behind me —

MULLALY [*reading over the top of him*]: "The domestic hardware industry is in a state of expansion. To cope with the upsurge in home building, factories are increasing their output. Typical figures for the year were: plastic canisters, half a million. Garden forks, one hundred thousand —

FLOCKHART [*clapping*]: Hurrah for the facts! The marvellous facts! They blind you in the end, like specks of sand. How much? How many? What's the percentage? What does it profit a man? What?

MULLALY : You know what the problem with you is? You've never *faced* the facts! You won't acknowledge the facts! Learn to live with them — or get out!

FLOCKHART : I'm going my friend, I'm going. The hours can't go quickly enough . . . but before I go, consider the hens!

MULLALY : To hell with the hens! I'm sick of hearing about hens!

FLOCKHART : The pathetic pitiful hens! Crowded into pens, kept under lights, egg-and-meat machines — who do we think we are? Hurrying up one natural cycle, putting a stop to another — we're like little boys with a great big clock. It's got to stop! Out with the lights! Off with the air-conditioning! Open the windows! Air! Air! Save us!

MULLALY : You're mad! Stark raving mad! You're not a research officer, you're a lunatic!

FLOCKHART : That's just it, don't you understand? It's because I've done all this calm, detached research year in year out — that's why it happened! For years I've assessed, tabulated, computed — without a foot in the real world! I'm *dying* of objectivity!

[*Door opens.*]

PRESNELL : I heard shouting. Is everything alright?

FLOCKHART : Quite alright Mr Presnell. Just a little Black Mass. We sacrifice Dolores at three. Presnell, d'you know you look like Beelzebub himself in your regalia? What's your trouble?

PRESNELL : There appears to be some irregularity in your application for moneys accruing in lieu of service leave.

FLOCKHART : Kindly address me in my native tongue Presnell.

"Moneys accruing in lieu of leave" — how that line sings. It's Tennyson, isn't it?

PRESNELL : It's the *Government Gazette* unfortunately, and it means what it says. You've claimed for the equivalent of five years service since your last leave. But for three months of that period you were off work.

FLOCKHART : I had a heart condition! Brought on by overwork!

PRESNELL [*laughing*]: Pardon my amusement. Overwork! Whatever the reason, you can't claim for it. Regulation 15 (c) states — " . . . in the eventuality of an officer —"

FLOCKHART : Stop, I confess, I'll sign anything. I can't bear to see an innocent language being tortured. By the way, I believe you took exception when the Social Club used the side of the tea urn for advertising purposes.

PRESNELL : And why not? If people in authority won't stick by the rules, what's going to happen? Anarchy in the streets, that's what — the violation of women, gangs of hooligans smashing shop windows, innocent motorists dragged from their vehicles —

FLOCKHART : Presnell, has it ever occurred to you that in your ill-fitting grey gunmetal suit you incarnate the forces of evil? Not on the grand scale perhaps. But when you add up all these little single-breasted evils, these logarithms of pettiness, you suffocate the world.

PRESNELL [*opening door*]: Yes. Bye bye Flockhart. We're all going to be sorry to see you go. It's going to be a painful time for all of us. Someone in the staff room likened it to releasing a ferret from its cage.

FLOCKHART : A ferret? How dare you sir! Good afternoon! Go!

[*Door slams shut.*]

[MULLALY *resumes tapping, somewhat uncertainly after this outburst.*]

. . . What a laugh . . . him in his nose and ears . . . like a constipated koala . . . wait till I hit 'em with my farewell speech . . . that'll put the cat amongst the pigeons . . . buk-buk-buk . . . bloody pecking order . . . buk-buk-buk- stop that.

MULLALY [*reading determinedly*]: "In the fields of laminated plastic veneers, the domestic hardware industry can be seen at its most vigorous" —

FLOCKHART : I was like you once. Fresh out of university, keen, ambitious — and then the minstrel boy got himself a Canberra job — and I settled behind a desk and sort of — faded away. So here I am, just two rungs up the ladder from where I started — and now — I'm jumping off!

MULLALY [*getting up and grabbing him*]: Don't jump! Don't jump!

FLOCKHART : Oh unhand me you idiot. I was speaking metaphorically — a word statisticians don't understand.

[*Tap-tap-tap of* MULLALY's *typewriter as he grimly forges on.*]

Soon they'll be here.

[*Tap-tap-tap.*]

They'll be along any time from now —

MULLALY : Won't you ever shut up? Who'll be here, who?

FLOCKHART : They. Them. The personnel. The nobodies. They'll come to bid me farewell and godspeed. Not that they want to — it's just that the regulations require it. They'll make a presentation and I will be able to speak to them — those buckpassers, those memo-spawners, those fancy footworkers in the files — and they'll have to stand there and listen. Hunter — Hunter above all. Bear with me while I tell you about Hunter, the man that beat me on appeal, the man —

MULLALY : I don't want to *hear* about Hunter! I'm not interested in Hunter!

FLOCKHART : I intend to tell you about Hunter for your own good!

MULLALY [*grimly*]: "The domestic hardware industry can be divided into four sections —"

FLOCKHART : Hunter! Here are the facts!

MULLALY [*picking up phone*]: Mr Simmons? Mullaly speaking. Look here, I'll simply have to change my room ... I see, yes ... I know he'll be gone tomorrow. It's a question of whether I can survive today —

[*Phone down.*]

FLOCKHART : You can't change your room, just like that. These things are fixed, eternal, Ptolemaic. Every part of this building has been carefully subdivided into sections, according to an elaborate formula involving status and length of service. Besides, there's no room to move into —

files fill the highways and the byways, like cows in India . . .
Hunter! The man who sold his shabby little soul for a piece
of green executive carpet! The man who crawled, wheedled,
pecked and flapped his way to the topmost — buk-buk-buk-
perch!

MULLAY : Right! Enough! I can't stand it anymore! You hate the
place — well, go, go, go!

FLOCKHART : Hush! I hear footfalls! They come my boy! Hear
their heavy tread, as they prepare to say the last rites over
Flockhart!

[*Bang of gong.*]

Come in, assassins of the *aide memoire* . . . prepare yourself
for the spectacle Mullaly. An officer is about to be ritually
retired. Gentlemen, what an honour. Come in, come in all
of you. Never have I had so many guests . . . and what is this
bringing up the rear — the Social Club Trio! I'm over-
whelmed!

[*Tap-tap of baton as if on rostrum; a quiet voice saying
one-two-three, one-two-three; then an air is rendered, light
and yet faintly menacing. Music swells, then fades.*]

VOICE : Gentlemen, the divisional head: Mr J.B. Hunter, Bachelor of Commerce, O.B.E., Fellow of the Australian Institute
of Accountants, Life Member of the Canberra Lawn Bowls
Association —

HUNTER : That's enough, that's enough. I thank you. Page one of
the handbook gentlemen: *Farewell Presentations*: and I
quote therefrom: "Where an officer is retiring, either
through illness or age, and he is known widely through the
department, a collection may be taken up, and the usual
presentation made. In such cases, a Grade Eight level gift is
the most apt — to wit: an item of local fauna or flora
embedded in clear plastic, boomerang shaped, to serve as
either ornament or ashtray" endquote. Before presenting
the superannuant with this object, could we have the official recital — Section One — Appropriate Sentiments. All
together now —

VOICES : Indeed a pleasure and a privilege. Stand before you on
this unhappy occasion. Had our little differences in the
past. Fresh fields we trust and pastures new. Pouring oil on

troubled waters. Take bull by the horns. No fool like an old fool. Dogs bark and the caravan passes on.

HUNTER : Good, good. There you are old chap. I'd like you to accept this gift as a token of our esteem. And indeed relief. Look at it! Not only decorative, but ideal for the smoker. It's yours Flockhart; see? Your initials are engraved on the base.

[*Discreet applause.*]

FLOCKHART : A tiny chicken! Preserved for ever in pure plastic — a kind of post-natal egg. Thank you, thank you. And now gentlemen, it's my turn — my speech, my speech — buk-buk-buk.

HUNTER : Unfortunately Flockhart, my time is short. I have a conference in ten minutes with the Controller on the loofah sponge and pig bristle industries —

FLOCKHART : My speech! I've worked for hours on it — gentlemen, I insist. I wish to address you briefly on the subject of the Australian Poultry Industry. You may not know it, but 208 birds arrived with the first fleet in 1788. From this small beginning there has arisen a thriving, clucking enterprise, producing — buk-buk-buk — some 4000 million eggs annually — eggs! eggs! Everywhere you look! —

HUNTER : Hurry up man! This is no time for an industry survey.

FLOCKHART : Gentlemen. Since your impatience is obvious, I will jump from the introduction of my speech, on which I spent hours, to the conclusion — which describes the time I actually met, in the flesh, the Minister!

HUNTER : Oh God, not again — I knew it, I knew it... biggest thing in his life... Come on then man, come on — quickly, quickly —

FLOCKHART : The Minister! His personal signature was all I needed, on an urgent document. Knowing how long it would take through the normal channels, a demon took possession of me, and I decided to take the lift up — to the Ministerial suite! I stepped out onto soft carpet, I knocked on his secretary's door, and the gods were with me — she was out! Beyond were the great gold doors, beyond which the Minister himself would be going about his mysterious and awesome affairs. Doubts assailed me, but I was — possessed! I knocked gently on the great crested panels —

and was bidden to enter! And there, at the end of a blue carpet, at his desk — the Minister, peering at me over his glasses! "Yes?" says he, "What's the trouble?" "A trifling matter my lord" I replied — "if you could grace this document with the perfume of your signature" — oh, I was eloquent before him — and as he signed, we had a cordial exchange about the weather. Then I bowed, and retreated, while he resumed his onerous tasks, already oblivious of my existence — or so I thought —

[*Sounds of impatience from his listeners.*]

— stay gentlemen, stay — because even as I descended to the lower levels, the Minister had lifted his phone to report my temerity to the Controller, who rang the Head of Department, who rang the Divisional Director — none other than you Mr Hunter, and you saw to it that I was punished. Gentlemen, you turn to go, but hear me out — for now — I curse the Minister, I say to hell with his hideous effigy up there on the wall, down with his nose, his ears, his everything!

[*Sounds of disturbances, dismay.*]

HUNTER : The sin against the Minister! Blasphemy! The penalty is death!

FLOCKHART : He's the guilty one you fools! Up there on the wall! That's where the poison comes from, drop by drop, from him into the entire organism! Pull down his pictures! Rip off the masks! Drain the poison! Down with him!

[*More sounds of disturbance.*]

HUNTER : The sin against the Minister! Seize him!

FLOCKHART [*being seized, to the background music of the "Rite of Spring"*]: Ooh — aah! Fools! Buk-buk-buk — you don't understand! Save me Mullaly, save me!

MULLALY : My god! What's going on? What are you doing to him? Let him go, let him go!

FLOCKHART [*still struggling*]: Never mind Mullaly, there's nothing you can do. Watch! Watch! See the partition slide back my boy? What do you see Mullaly, what do you see?

MULLALY : Good lord — a-a Continuous Line Poultry-Killing Apparatus, labelled at each stage! Plucking — Slaughtering — Scalding — Eviscerating — Spraying — Chilling — Despatch! Oh my God!

FLOCKHART : Exactly my boy, exactly! I have sinned against the Minister — for which there is no forgiveness! See? They hang me upside down — like Saint Peter —

MULLALY : Oh my God! I've got to get out of here! What's happening?

FLOCKHART : Stay Mullaly — remind others after I have gone that it was Flockhart who pioneered poultry research. My barnyard friends will revenge me, I can see it now! Eggs, eggs, raining down upon the earth in their millions, volcanic and terrible! Buk-buk-buk —

HUNTER : Pluck him — down to his undergarments. Then have it done decently and with despatch, in accordance with the regulations!

MULLALY : This is madness! Put the man down! Put him down!

FLOCKHART : It's too late Mullaly. Feed my pullets, feed my hens!

HUNTER : On! On to the next stage! To the — Slaughtering!

[FLOCKHART *expires with a cry, followed by sounds of thunder, mechanical conveyors, and a flurry of buk-buks and wings.*]

Let the tea trolley be brought in for removal of the remains when they reach Despatch —

[*Sounds of various processing noises.*]

MULLALY : Out! I must get out!

HUNTER : And let the official litany be said. All together now —

MULLALY : — The door, quickly!

HUNTER : Cattle for slaughter.

VOICES [*in response*]: Pray for us.

HUNTER : Beef, with or without bones.

VOICES : Pray for us.

MULLALY : The door! Please God they haven't locked the door!

HUNTER : Liver of animals.

VOICES : Pray for us.

HUNTER : Tongues, hearts, kidneys, tails.

VOICES : Pray for us.

MULLALY [*opening door*]: Saved! At last!

HUNTER [*receding*]: Tripe, dehydrated.

VOICES [*receding*]: Pray for us.

HUNTER [*receding*]: Other giblets not named.

VOICES : Pray for us.

MULLALY [*to himself*]: I've got to get back to Melbourne!

Scanlan

CHARACTER

SCANLAN: a lecturer in English, middle-aged

The set should suggest a seminar situation: a long table, surrounded by empty chairs. Flask of water and glass. At each side of the head of the table, at a moderate distance, large potted ferns. Above the head of the table hangs a large picture of the nineteenth-century Australian poet Henry Kendall.

Enter SCANLAN, *a middle-aged academic in a middle-aged academic suit. He's obviously late, and looks somewhat disoriented and hard-pressed. He carries a bulging briefcase, which he puts on the table and unpacks as he starts his lecture.*

SCANLAN : Permit me to apologize, ladies and gentlemen, for my late arrival. I missed my plane by a matter of minutes, dashing into the airport just as it was preparing to take off. It's a rhetorical question, but I'm still going to ask it: is there anything so irrevocable as an aircraft narrowly missed? But miss it I did, and the next hour was spent cooling my heels in the terminal building. Terminal. As in illness. The air overheated, the music piped, the lights fluorescent, the ears harried by public announcements, the thirst slaked by liquor excessively priced. The road to hell, paved with vinyl tiles and fruit-fly inspectors.

But now the journey is over, and what an honour it is to stand before such a distinguished assemblage, amongst whom I note some old friends — [*bowing to each*] Professor McGiff, still hearty and hale at eighty, Dr Williams making light of her calipers, Mr Gelly obviously recovered from his stroke, and my old colleague Dr Grigsby, whom apparently we have to thank for organizing this seminar, and [*looking at Grigsby's chair with guarded suspicion*] who was responsible, I have only just discovered, for my receiving an invitation, though it is not his signature that appears at the base of the letter . . . [*trailing off mysteriously, as if suspecting a plot*].

And now, I can delay no longer. I can put off no more the moment when I must leave my burrow and show my ears above the grass. Prime your fowling pieces ladies and gentlemen, release the hounds, send the beaters forward — Scanlan is out and running! . . . Henry Kendall and the Poetry of Possibility. Or, Henry Kendall and the Forests of the Heart . . . or, Henry Kendall and the Metrics of Ambiguity . . . or the Prosody of Pain . . . or the Dactyls of Defeat . . . or, Henry Kendall: Bo Diddley or Baudelaire . . . [*muttering*] that should just about please everyone . . . Of those among you who are wondering why my subject is a nineteenth-century poet, delivered at a seminar devoted to twentieth-century Australian literary issues, I request patience. I must ask you to [*making odd paw — and — claw — gestures with the hands*] bear with me. . . . Despite the conventional wisdom to the contrary, despite Dr Grigsby's printed opinion that our poet is no more than Wordsworth and water, I propose to show that, far from being a mere Victorian versifier, Henry Kendall is in fact a harbinger of our present age.

First, a speedy background sketch. [*Suddenly standing and plucking*] A date, from the palm-trees of history! Eighteen thirteen — the crossing of the — ? [*looking around, schoolmasterish, for suggestions*] yes, over there — Blue Mountains! Correct. And the men who did it, who sound collectively like a firm of solicitors, were as you know Blaxland, Lawson, and Wentworth . . . . [*Musing*] A *firm* of solicitors . . . surely there is a more appropriate collective noun . . . a weakness of solicitors . . . a pride of lions and a humiliation of barristers — I'm sorry. Lecturing to students is one thing. Performing before one's peers is another. The result is nervousness, dryness of the throat, attempts to retrieve the situation with whimsy. I take sedatives on medical advice.

[*Produces suspicious-looking flask and drinks from it with odd furtive movement while trying to distract his audience by gesturing toward the Kendall portrait with blackboard pointer.*]

understood that his relationship wit
one, that he is in fact a poet of
pondences, that his art engages in
[*miming an outward movement*] p
onto nature in an outward thrust
inward movement] internalizing t
same time . . . . It is in the light of this
once and threshing about] symbioti
should be considered . . . . You want
give you chapter and verse.
[*Turning round and looking up at p*
that has to be placated]
　　From the runs of the Narran, wide
　　And loud with the lowing of cattle
　　We speed for a Land where the str
　　And the hidden creeks bubble and
[*Looking round quickly*]
Dr Grigsby? I'd know that laugh any
last word amusing? You feel no p
versifier, who, having had the misfo
word *cattle* in an *a b a b* quatrain, find
in difficulties in line four? Yes — the l
and brattle. And why not? There are
disposal — prattle, rattle, battle, tat
these easy solutions, the poet opts to
alliterative neologism that is highly
[*Pouring a drink and listening clos*
Brattling!
[*Drinks.*]
But what do we care about the car
academics? To our horses!
[*Reading with galloping fervou*
increasingly equestrian as he does do]
　　Now call on the horses, and leave th
　　And sources of rivers that all of us l
　Three rhymes, Grigsby, in a line and a
　　For, crossing the ridges, and passing
　　And running up gorges, we'll come t
　　Of gullies where waters eternally flo
Half rhymes and eye rhymes and blin

Handsome fellow, very handsome.
[*Refreshed, lubricated, and unwittingly making it apparent that it's not the first drink he's had that day*] Eighteen thirteen, and the Blue Mountains crossed and the limitless vistas beyond . . . [*Ferreting among his papers*] If I could quote from one authority on the subject . . . . "What was the cause of this expansion? The thirst of British manufacturers for wool [*sucking at his coatsleeve uncontrollably, then quickly getting a grip on himself*] and the hunger of Australian farmers for land [*brief biting and snapping with the jaws*] very soon outran [*jogging on the spot*] the narrow hinterland of Sydney." [*still jogging*] And what do we descry, as we cross those blue peaks? To the west, the eternal horizontals of the plains . . . to the north and south, the ageless verticals of the rainforests! Forests where the new generation were also to take root and rise up, straight and tall as the gums! [*Stops jogging.*]

It must be remembered that up until this time Australian verse did no more than [*strange simian arm-movements*] ape English models . . . As the natives delighted in cast-off top hats and jackets, so too did our earliest versifiers make themselves foolish by dressing themselves in the trappings of a Pope or a Johnson . . . . Listen, for example, to W.C. Wentworth's "Australia" — note the relentlessly heavy Augustan hand: [*As he reads, his hands become heavier, forcing the page down, pressing harder and harder against the tabletop.*]
　　And, oh Britannia! Shouldst thou cease to ride
　　Despotic Empress of old Ocean's tide . . . .
　　May this, thy last-born infant, then arise
[*Ironical fortissimo.*]
　　To glad thy heart and greet thy parents' eyes;
　　And Australasia float, with flag unfurl'd
　　A new Britannia in another world!
It was this conventional sensibility that the new breed of currency-lad poets, Charles Harpur and Henry Kendall, decisively rejected. They set themselves the daunting task of reinterpreting the continent in the light of the new romantic temper — it was they who pioneered that long struggle to absorb and render the alien Australian land-

scape [*reaching out to whac
pointer*] — a struggle that co

And so — *pace* Dr Grigsby
Henry Kendall is [*ferreting, t*
"confined by diction, prosod
bourgeois velvet cell of his ow
matter is that Kendall opens
them . . . . It is Kendall that op
majesty and mystery of Nature
vegetation dense and dark, tho
closer, prowling, stalking [*app
pointer as if about to impale a
and becoming entangled*] — t
nothing — breathing, alive, lu:
closer — while we sit here
[*Picking himself up from u
ferns*] It's all right for the En
with their landscape for cent
shaped, polished it till they can
for us — within an arm's lengtl
[*Pausing for a breath and a d*
If my conduct appears excessiv
apologize — I've been under stra
an overwhelming sense of loss,
inner being had been extracted
asleep and I am now left with li
I'm participating in a shadov
meaningless ritual, as if some ce
away and I wake each mor
increasingly shapeless sack of n
deprived of this shaping spirit th
year but by the hour, the hair grey
pouching and wrinkling as I stare
still believes in my existence is r
endless war of attrition against r
that I am not already vanquishe
shrug, a tone of voice, an opinion
[*Regaining thread*]
So — let us hear no more about
nineteenth-century painter and c

say this man is a nobody — you who have never even ridden a horse, never dared anything, never felt the wind in your face!
[*Reading and riding faster*]
The leagues we may travel down beds of hot gravel,
And clay-rusted reaches where moisture hath been,
While searching for waters may vex us and thwart us,
Yet who would be quailing, or fainting, or failing?
Not you who are sons of the Narran, I — ween.
Yes, *ween*. Chuckle away. It wasn't considered so funny a hundred years ago, my friend, I assure you — Wordsworth used it — Shelley — Keats — in those days *everybody* was weening!
[*Pause, drinks.*]
My throat's so dry — my nerves — [*to Grigsby*] I know your game — I know what you're up to. It's not Kendall you're mocking, it's me. You find it amusing that I have devoted my life to a nonentity, is that it? Well, my good friend and ladies and gentlemen, I see it otherwise — it is I, not you, that have the task, the challenge — I've been called, required, obligated, to defend the gentle garden of Henry Kendall — I keep the lines straight, the plots neat, the colours and images well watered — I weed, delve, prune — but every so often a herbivore escapes from the herd, pushes in the gate and gets inside, grunting, tossing, trampling [*pointing the pointer at Grigsby, and flourishing an imaginary cape matador-fashion*] — but I'll have you out of here before the hour's up — you and all the other snorters and bellowers — one day my faith in Henry Kendall will be — [*extending his arms, assuming a crucified posture*] redeemed! He will be recognized for the poet that he is — apologies will be made — revaluations, pilgrimages, bouquets of flowers, articles in the Saturday pages — he will be raised up on high, and I, like the good thief, will accompany him into his kingdom!
[*Pause.*]
And the Grigsbys of this world will come pleading for a drop of water!
[*Drinks.*]
I'm sorry, I speak excessively, wax vehement . . . . I'm tired,

if you want the truth of the matter . . . . I slept badly, haunted by the thought that upon my performance here today my reputation, for what it is worth, stands or falls . . . and yet my wife has conceived the remarkable notion that seminars such as these are pretexts, that once the preliminaries are disposed of, middle-aged academics such as myself home in on the nearest attractive woman in the gathering, follow her scent, stalk her behind the tea urn, and fall upon her in a shower of sugar cubes and biscuits . . . . Accordingly . . . my wife — my wife Margaret — took measures to prevent my departure. I found, on dressing this morning, I had no belt for my trousers, but this proved a disguised blessing, helping as it did to conceal the fact that she'd hidden away virtually every sock I had to my name. . . .

It is a disservice nevertheless to any artist to praise him over and beyond his due merits. And since we find ourselves fallen amongst Kendall's bush ballads, some discriminations are therefore in order . . . . If these poems, lively as they are, are compared with the rough popular songs that precede them, or the work of Gordon and Paterson that comes after, it will be seen that our poet —
[*Weary after a bout of peripatetic lecturing, he goes to sit down, misses the chair, almost falls to the floor.*]
— falls between two stools . . . failing as he does to recapture the crude earthy vigour of the former, while at the same time too poetical to attain the lively narrative drive of the latter . . . . Kendall indeed was an intensely self-conscious and literary writer. Not for him the easy familiarity of —
[*Bursting into song*]
   'tis of a wild colonial boy, Jack Doolan was his name,
   Of poor but honest parents, he was born in Castlemaine.
   He was his father's only hope, his mother's only joy,
   And dearly did his parents love the wild colonial boy.
— with its rough-hewn hearty spontaneities and rollicking choruses —
[*Sings again, louder.*]
   Come, all me hearties, we'll roam the mountains high,
   Together we will plunder, together we will die.

We'll wander over valleys, and gallop over plains,
    And we'll scorn to live in slavery —
[*Breaking off*] Phew. The heat.
[*Takes off jacket, revealing ragged shirt. Regards it ruefully.*]
So determined was my dear wife that I should be spared the carnal delights of the seminar that my shirts were left unwashed, which is why I appear before you in a garment usually reserved for weekend gardening . . . . It is Kendall's love of description, his fondness for figure and trope that lead him to overlay his ballads with an elaboration that makes them hybrids — neither [*momentary swimming movements*] the fish of ballad nor [*flapping movements*] the fair lyric fowl — thus [*reciting*]:
    When the thunder ceases pealing, and the stars up heaven are stealing,
    And the moon above us wheeling throws her pleasant glances round —
[*Flapping again*] Not quite lyrical fowl — and not quite the authentic piscian article either . . . . phew. So hot!
[*Loosens tie, undoes some shirt buttons, exposing a Puffing Billy Preservation Society T-shirt, which again he inspects ruefully before proceeding.*]
What a strange little family — husband, wife, and one introverted adolescent son, a loner, a brooder, whose one passion in life is railways. Trains all over his walls, speeding, shunting, steaming . . . timetables, brochures, and esoteric books on forgotten narrow gauges deep in the timberlands . . . . Last summer I painted the ceiling of his room. Ignorant as I am of practical matters, I applied the new paint directly over the old . . . . Every time the door is opened or closed a strange thing happens — a tiny shower of white paint-specks falls, fine as dandruff, on him, his bed, his books . . . . Kendall always aspired to write a long narrative poem but never succeeded, perhaps because of the difficulties he encountered in his personal life. Plagued by money worries, tempted by the twin demons of self-pity and alcohol, he never seemed to find time for anything other than short lyrical outbursts . . . .

[*Bursts uncontrollably into high-pitched song, then checks himself.*]

Indeed, the fact must be faced, in any treatment of his life and work, that Kendall had many weaknesses, and drink was one of them — but this scarcely justifies the following [*ferreting about for quote*]: "In April 1872 Kendall finally succumbed to the chronic instability and weakness of will that had always plagued him. Abandoned by his muse, his wife, and his family, he wandered the streets and slept in the gutters of Sydney, saturated in alcohol — a condition for which he had no one to blame but himself". This is Dr Grigsby's final and pitiless conclusion to the article to which I have already referred — an article which dismisses in four pages the labours of two lives — not only the poet's, but also, if I may be permitted to say so, my own . . . . Dr Grigsby is seemingly unaware of the difficulties of colonial life for the sensitive person, and the special difficulties it held for the artist . . . . For the handful of poets who practised their art at the time, suicide was the rule rather than the exception — such was the raw hurly-burly of frontier existence . . . .

[*Musing*]

Remarkable the number of compound words suggesting confusion all beginning with aitch — hurly-burly, hocus-pocus, higgledy-piggledy . . . . There were good reasons for Kendall's periodic attempts to seek refuge in drink — hotch-potch, there's another — though Kendall's volume *Leaves from Australian Forests* was well received, it failed financially — holus-bolus, that's a fifth — leaving him in desperate straits — harum-scarum, a sixth — then, when his baby daughter took ill and died, he blamed himself — wait, helter-skelter, there's dozens of 'em — hugger-mugger, hanky-panky, hurdy-gurdy —

[*Starts to wander, as if lost, in circles, getting giddy.*]

— hurdy gurdy — hurdy gurdy — hurdy gurdy — is it any wonder he wandered the Sydney streets lost and ill, eventually succumbing — hurdy gurdy — hurdy gurdy — to [*losing his balance and falling*] complete nervous collapse.

[*Dragging himself clear of the table, then dealing briskly,*

still prone, with an apparent attempt to stop his lecture]
No sir, I won't be interrupted — I have the floor.
[*Reciting, with a mixture of sadness and defiance*]
    But Sorrow speaks in singing leaf,
    And trouble talketh in the tide;
    The skirts of a stupendous grief
    Are travelling ever at my side

    The world is round me with its heat
    And toil, and cares that tire:
    I cannot with my feeble feet
    Climb after my desire.
[*Lifting himself up, wary but determined, and pointing to Grigsby*]
You want to bring Kendall down and me with him. That's your plan. That's why you had me invited here today. Every man has his time of darkness — knowing that mine was upon me, you lured me here, hiding behind the signature of a functionary, hoping you had supplied enough rope for me to hang myself publicly.... You really think four contemptible pages in an obscure quarterly [*pointing to Kendall photo*] will bring us down? Four pages of polemic, ridicule, rhetoric, innuendo, calumny, detraction, contumely, begging of questions, a prioris, argumentum ad hominem, pathetic fallacies, undistributed middles....
[*Regaining thread*]
Not even Kendall's finest lyric achievement is safe from Grigsby's flailing haymakers and knees to the groin. In his headlong jump to his foolish conclusion, the exquisite "Bell-birds" is dealt a flurry of kicks and punches on the way.... Kendall is attacked, if you please, for claiming that the notes of the bellbird are "softer than slumber" [*first uncontrollable tinkle or trill*] when they are allegedly a staccato tinkling [*second trill*]. Dr Grigsby is up to his usual trick of lifting a poetic phrase out of context, thus depriving it of symbolic resonance. Let us put this crystalline expression back in the jewelled setting where it belongs —
[*Recites.*]
    By channels of coolness the echoes are calling,
    And down the dim gorges I hear the creek falling;

[*Another trilling outburst.*]
    It lives in the mountain, where moss and the sedges
    Touch with their beauty the banks and the ledges;
[*Through the rest of the poem he fights the impulse, managing finally to get it under control.*]
    Through brakes of the cedar and sycamore bowers
    Struggles the light that is love to the flowers.
    — And *softer than slumber*, and sweeter than singing,
    The notes of the bell-birds are running and ringing.
— a combination of pictures, personal feeling and [*final brief trill*] music that taken together represent a pioneering assimilation of the Australian landscape into poetry.

Yes, Dr Grigsby, he wrote as a Victorian with Wordsworth and Tennyson as models. Yes, he was often guilty of sentimentality and even bathos — but he had at his best, rare moments the pure gift of song — and that is what matters. To hear "Mooni", one of his finest lyrics, spoken by one of our finest actors, will I think, drive my point home.

[*Switches on tape-recorder. Sounds of* SCANLAN *and his wife in somewhat heated argument. Listens mutely, resignedly for a few moments before switching it off.*]
I'm sorry. My son, even my son, is also at odds with me . . . . he has developed a sado-masochistic habit of covertly recording our marital disagreements, and has inserted this somehow on the tape . . . .
[*Presses button, runs tape for a few seconds at high speed, stops, switches it on again. This time, sounds of savage, almost hysterical argument. Turns it off, and faces Grigsby*]
Music to your ears. Bliss. All your own work . . . . The moment you discovered myself and your poor wife red-handed, *in flagrante*, you told *my* wife, and I've been paying for it ever since. One would have thought that would have been revenge enough for you — but no, not you . . . not content with wrecking two — no three — lives, you pursue me, stricken as I am, into the garden of verse. But that was a mistake — you didn't reckon that your victim, trapped, driven to desperation at being cornered in this last retreat,

would finally turn against his tormentor and show his teeth!

[*Regaining thread*]

There are indications that Kendall toyed with the idea of a narrative poem set on the mythical island of Tenna. In response to a letter from Henry Halloran in 1878, urging him to write such a poem, he replied —

[*Ferreting through his papers, picking up one after the other, and finally settling on one, which he reads as from a diary*]

February. Returned this day from bird-watching holiday at the Promontory. Fifteen different species in five days. Notebooks filled. Photographs taken. Friendship firmed. Confidences exchanged over campfire under a sky smoking and crackling with stars.... Poor Grigsby tells me he is unhappily married .... several cans of beer later I tell him I am too ....

[*Puts page down, picks up another*]

To Halloran's letter, the poet replied: "The long poem you wish me to write would require more leisure than that at present under my command. I have to work very hard, and my labour sometimes runs deep into the night."

[*Puts down page, picks up another.*]

April. Barbecue at Yarra Bend. Chops overcooked, claret raw.... [*looking at Grigsby*] Keen to show your old-public-school skills with the sculls, you suggest we hire a dinghy for a sally down river. Room for five only. You go with the children and Margaret — while your wife and I volunteer to stay behind. As your craft, expertly handled, proceeds round the bend, Sylvia and I ... Sylvia and I, both deprived, famished, crying out for ....

[*Regaining thread*]

In his early years Kendall produced a number of rather conventional love poems. Though their metrication is agreeable and the language never less than apt, these works have a certain mechanical quality.... As the years passed, however, and his experience deepened, there is a corresponding increase in the passion of his poetry ....

May, June, July.... happy times. Whenever Dr Grigsby is lecturing and I happen to be free, I visit my beloved Sylvia,

who waits for me, just a short walk away, scented with
pomades and lotions .... I leave my room, cross the
campus lawns. My blood pumps hard and high with
expectation, excitement seems to lift me off the ground, I
skim the grass weightless — I look for an analogue, a
correlative of my desire, and lo! it appears, as if I've created
it, summoned it up, beyond the trees — the spiked dome of
Newman College, something rare, exotic, tropical, from
Mexico perhaps or even Byzantium ....
[*Regaining thread*]
An added richness of tone, an intenser passion, is found in
Kendall's second volume of verse — and though to us today
such poems as "A Spanish Love Song" and "Campaspe"
seem harmless enough, to the Victorians they appeared out-
spoken and bold. George Smithers, reviewing this
particular volume in the *Colonial Monthly*, has this to say:
"Kendall's love knows nothing of chastity or purity — it is a
[*gradually becoming affected, meditative, because of the
erotic implications of the words*] wild hot foaming
passion ... libidinous in thought, and preying solely upon
physical beauty .... he invests the female form with a
sumptuousness of beauty which kindles the pulse as you
read it .... he makes his women Cleopatras in the ... im-
passioned suggestiveness of their physique .... these are
not the women of love but of lust .... such women as these
are not, we hope, destined to be the daughters and wives of
the future generations of Australians .... "
[*Slumps in his seat.*]
We — incandesced, every time we touched one another ...
she in her bath-robe of crimson towelling.... We rid ourselves of our clothes and then, at certain magical times, of
our bodies as well ... the drapes drawn ... loving in noon
darkness ... flying blind ... ecstatic levitations ... hawk-
like soarings ... sweet, gentle descents ... soft landings on
unknown fields .... we sailed, we voyaged, we rounded
capes, we beached, climbed hills, leapt off cliffs, swam,
sank, swirled — and there, as we lay together at five
fathoms, was Dr Grigsby standing at the door .... He was
supposed to be lecturing on the beginnings of the novel and
the rising middle classes .... [*to Grigsby*] You were very

strong on the middle classes ... they were always coming
up in your lectures ... whenever there was a painting or a
play or a novel, there they were, rising, rising ....
[*Regaining thread*]
It is in *Leaves from Australian Forests* that we find
Kendall's most sustained love lyric, an elegy, beautifully
turned, passionately felt, in memory of his disappointed
love for Rose Barnett —

But Rose Lorraine — ah, Rose Lorraine,
I'll whisper now where no one hears.
If you should chance to meet again
The man you kissed in soft dead years, ...

[*Pause. Brief reverie. He wanders the stage a little, as if
searching.*]

If I that breathe your slow sweet name
As one breathes low notes on a flute ....

— Sylvia? Sylvia? [*At Grigsby*] You'd bided your time,
ducked out of your lecture, and slipped back to the house,
leaving the rising middle classes suspended twenty feet in
the air. You gave me fifteen minutes start, then came after
me, creeping down the sideway, sneaking in the back
door ... insinuating yourself along the hallway, perhaps on
all fours ... then you paused and no doubt you listened, you
heard our noises as we drowned, then — then — you opened
the door — slowly, and saw me trespassing in your garden,
entangled on your floral bedspread — I saw you as if
through water, you were there for only a second, an
apparition, not looking, your eyes lowered as if the submarine light stung them — then you closed the door gently,
for all the world like an intruding butler.
[*Regaining*]
Despite the efforts of the respectable to suggest the
contrary, it was undoubtedly Rose Barnett that was
Kendall's great love and *not* his wife Charlotte, who
admittedly had much to contend with in living with so
sensitive and wayward a man ....
You closed the door quietly and discreetly, as if you'd
discovered us both sound asleep .... You walked back to
the university, where by now the wretched middle classes
lay all over the grass like a crumpled balloon, you went to

your office and — you rang my wife. [*As if quelling an
interruption from Grigsby*] Yes — I don't deny it was all
very upsetting — but ringing my wife was hardly the action
of a person who's upset — it was a cold and calculated
action, a cruel and deliberate action. But you calculated
badly — it was just what Margaret wanted to hear, it
proved once and for all that I was the worthless, faithless,
degenerate creature she had always believed me to be . . . so
your strategy failed . . . . Her contempt for me, your
contempt for Sylvia drove us closer together, made us more
hopeless, more desperate . . . . We promised you both that
we'd never meet — and went on meeting!
[*Regaining*]
Kendall's eldest son wrote of him thus: "All Kendall's
petulant excuses for his own lapses and failings, his unfortunate itch to throw upon his nearest and dearest the
blame for his own faults, should not be taken as justified.
His very action in living so long with his wife should help at
least in part to cancel the shame of what he calls his
irresponsible moments. . . ."
We met in parks, in cars, in the basements of buildings, the
flats of friends. . . . You tried another tactic. You used the
last weapon you had — your children. You got leave from
the university and you took them away from her. . . . She
was torn between them and me, she was a woman halved,
quartered. . . . To stop her being pulled apart, I let her
go. . . .
    Nevertheless, Kendall's love for Rose Barnett was deep
and abiding. The depth of his sorrow when his romance
with her was finally broken haunts "Farewell", one of his
finest poems —
    And part we thus? The spell is broken
    On thee my thoughts no more may dwell
    And all that now remains is spoken
    In this sad simple word "Farewell".

    We meet no more! And thus shall perish
    The dreams, the hopes, that once were mine
    And memory may not dare to cherish
    One gentle look or smile of thine.

The saddest and the tenderest token
Of my despair words may not tell
For all — for all —
I gave her up.... You forced me out of her garden.... Wounded, I crept into his [*pointing to Kendall's picture*] ... green dreams, flowered images ... and you — you pursued me even there — seeking the death-blow, you followed me.... You lured me out with an invitation, knowing that it was my own dark time ... she in another city ... my own now alien to me ... my wife's prickings and kickings....

Darkness descends on me ... attacks of nerves, depression, irritability ... bouts of drinking, incoherence at late afternoon lectures, a fall down the steps of the Arts Building.... To ensure my final humiliation before the academic world, you arrange to have me invited here today.... I take the bait, not realizing it was your doing until it was too late ... hoping to regain my footing, longing to retrieve all, to plumb as it were the caverns of the imagination before an admiring audience of my peers.... A speleologist, that's what I'd be, exploring depths no one has yet ventured ... underground lakes, subterranean auroras, irridescent wall paintings ... the waters rising, but I would surface in time to applause, and tell of amazing discoveries ... the waters rising, threatening to cut me off ... the air growing more and more foul, dank, unbreathable ...

[*Lights slowly down.*]

The darkness closing in, my tugs on the rope going unanswered ... harder to breathe — darker — darker.... Henry Kendall — his lamp, his lifeline to the real world, his poem entitled "Beyond Kerguelen", the remotest island on earth, admired by Oscar Wilde ... extraordinary performance ... never be invited again ... time of darkness — no light and no tunnel ... signed his early works Henry Kendall NAP, which stood for Native Australian Poet.... Sylvia? Sylvia?

[*Darkness.*]

The Great God Mogadon

Mogadon

A Radio Play

CHARACTERS

EDWARD SEARLE : a middle-aged bachelor
ANDERSON : a government official
KEEFE : a government official
VOICE COACH
JOHNSON : the Prime Minister's valet
LAMPEDUSA : a PR man
OLD LADY
LORD MAYOR

Running-up-a-flight-of-stairs sounds, with out-of-breath puffing. A door is opened suddenly and closed. More puffing. As the puffer gets his breath back, he talks to himself with a familiarity that suggests he's a loner who often engages in such conversations. He's talking to himself in incredulous whispers.

SEARLE : If they saw me — if I'm spotted — kaputt.... they couldn't have seen you — how could they see you in the dark?... fool that you are — bloody fool — walked right into it.... come on, come on, get yourself together! Compose yourself! Compose, that's the word! Write it down! Leave a message! Tell the world! Otherwise, who's going to know? You're a nothing! That's why they picked on you, you poor fool! Because you're a nothing! A little middle-aged bachelor with halitosis and dandruff.... if you don't write it down — and they find you here — you'll just — disappear! And nobody'll know about Mister Nobody!... pen! Paper! Quickly!
[*Composing and writing*] My name is Edward Searle. I live — reside perhaps — reside or live? Oh, hurry up, hurry up — I *exist* at flat 6, 18 Forrest Avenue, Canberra.... when was it, when?... on Sunday, Sunday night — where are we now, Tuesday night or early hours of Wednesday morning, that's it — on Sunday August the fourteenth, just before midnight, when I was sound asleep — I'd taken a Mogadon, don't sleep well, medical advice — I was well away, deep in dreamless slumber, snug under the blankets, curled up and warm as a baby, when I was awakened by what appeared to be knocking at my front door —

[*Soft knocking, as if penetrating the sleeping consciousness, quickly getting louder.*]

My God, it *is* knocking!

[*We cross to actual event being described.*]

My God, who? On a Sunday? At midnight?

[*More knocks, he shuffles and mumbles, then opens door.*]

You come round at this hour, to talk religion?

ANDERSON : Mister Edward Searle?

SEARLE : Yes, and I'm not at home — not to Mormons, Jehovah's Witnesses, or anybody.

ANDERSON : Sorry to disturb you so late —

SEARLE : Twelve ten, to be exact. Ten past twelve on a Sunday night — there's a time and a place for the word of God.

ANDERSON : It's an intrusion, I know, but we'd like to speak to you about an important matter.

SEARLE : To me? About an important matter?

ANDERSON : Affecting the national interest.

SEARLE : Wrong man, gentlemen, wrong man. You want Mr *Earle,* the Deputy Secretary of the Department — you want Earle, not Searle — two floors up with a view over the lake. A clerk, that's all I am, my friends — a senior clerk perhaps, but essentially a nobody, wrapped in the arms of Mogadon —isn't that a marvellous name for a sleeping pill? Mogadon. The great dinosaur of sleep. You've driven him away tonight, that's for certain.

ANDERSON [*unrelenting*] : My name is Anderson, and this is my colleague Mr Keefe.

SEARLE : Delighted. Two floors up.

KEEFE : The man we're after is called Searle, not Earle, and he lives at this address. Aged forty-five, height five feet ten, balding, a senior clerk in the Department of Works —

ANDERSON : — who used, when younger, to take a lively interest in theatre.

SEARLE : Amateur theatre. Me, unmistakably me. But gentlemen,

KEEFE : We — came across your photograph. We were looking for someone suitable, and we came across — this.

SEARLE : From my passport! Hardly flattering, specially when you blow it up like that —

KEEFE : Here's your photograph, and here's another.

SEARLE : The Prime Minister!

KEEFE : Ill.

SEARLE : Ill?

KEEFE : Gravely.

SEARLE : So that's why — for the last couple of weeks — no appearances.

ANDERSON : Normally it would be bad enough. But in times like these, a catastrophe.

SEARLE : Inflation soaring, unemployment everywhere, marches through the streets, pitched battles — no need to tell *me*.

ANDERSON : Troubled times. And that's why we're here. You can help us — heal them.

SEARLE : Me?

KEEFE : You. Watch. I take a felt pen of silver, and I put —
[*Squeaky felt pen sounds.*]

SEARLE : — wavy grey curls on my bald pate.
[*More sounds.*]

KEEFE : And again, on the chin —

SEARLE [*still not with it*] : — a trim little goatee beard . . .

ANDERSON [*triumphantly*] : And what do we have Mr Searle, what do we have?

SEARLE [*realizing*] : The likeness is — remarkable!

ANDERSON : The Prime Minister, Mr Searle. We have the Prime Minister —

KEEFE : — who at this very moment lies gravely ill.

SEARLE [*again realizing*] : But — I'm shorter than the right honourable gentlemam.

KEEFE : Platform soles.

SEARLE : Our voices — my somewhat nasal delivery — compared to — his modulations — a humble clerk —

KEEFE : A humble clerk with wide theatrical experience. Six years with the Adelphi Players, four with the Shakespeare Society, and I quote — "As Malvolio, Mr Edward Searle acquitted himself most creditably. Despite a certain awkwardness of gesture and physique, there can be no doubt that he is a mimic born."

SEARLE : Five years ago — a review in an obscure suburban newspaper, a throwaway —

KEEFE : — acquitted himself most creditably —

ANDERSON : — a mimic born.

SEARLE : I can't.

ANDERSON and KEEFE : You must.

ANDERSON : His Excellency is ill, gravely ill.

KEEFE : But this must not be discovered by the people.

ANDERSON : Civil disturbances, loss of public confidence, riots, commotions — the rending of the entire social fabric. Once it starts, there's no stopping —

SEARLE : The social fabric? Gentlemen, what has the social fabric to do with me?

ANDERSON : We're asking you, as a citizen, in the national interest

KEEFE : We request.

ANDERSON : — implore

KEEFE : — insist.

SEARLE : On what, for the love of God. What is it you want me to do?

ANDERSON : Prime Minister.

KEEFE : You.

ANDERSON : For a day.

KEEFE : A series of public appearances

ANDERSON : For a single day

KEEFE : For the sake of —

ANDERSON : — your country!

SEARLE [*weakly*] : I don't believe it.

ANDERSON and KEEFE [*quietly*] : But everyone else will . . . .

[*Sounds of computers, whirring tapes.*]

SEARLE [*to himself, half incredulous, half caught up in the situation*] : Nine o'clock Monday morning. The language laboratory. Speech practice! [*Practising a speech, half in his normal voice, half in Prime Ministerial modulations*]: Who Calls These Troubled Times? That, gentlemen, is the question I wish to speak about tonight, but before I do so —

VOICE COACH : — no, no, no! I see your tactics, Mr Searle. Your ploy is perfectly evident. However and nevertheless — I am fully aware of your abilities, and it is no use pretending you don't possess them. I will replay His Excellency's voice a third time —

PRIME MINISTER'S VOICE : I wish to express my appreciation to the people of Australia for exercising their rights of democratic choice in favour of myself and my party in such an overwhelming manner. You have placed your trust in me, in us, and I for·one do not propose to allow that trust —

VOICE COACH [*switching off tape*] : Now, Mr Searle, decide for yourself. Will you give us your best? We're going to stay here all day until you do. "Who Calls These Troubled Times?" Let's hear it!

SEARLE [*almost perfect*] : Who Calls These Troubled Times? That, gentlemen, is the question I wish to speak about tonight, but before I do so —

VOICE COACH: — better Mr Searle, better, but still not good enough. Breathe deeper, get the tongue right round these vowels, let the words roll out, rich and round —

SEARLE : Who Calls These Troubled Times? That, gentlemen, is the question . . . .

[*His voice trails off into a medley of sounds, a mix of his old voice, his new voice, his coach's voice and whirring tapes — all suggesting an exhausting quest for perfection.*]

[*To himself*] Again and again and again, until I was perfect . . . but that was only the beginning — for the rest of the day I was — Pygmalioned! I was bewigged and be-whiskered, manicured and bathed, sauna'd and scented, bespoke in the finest wools, tied in silk, socked in cashmere, shod in leather soft as gloves, platformed in subtle inch-and-a-half soles, wined, dined, until, at eight o'clock in the evening, goateed, barbered, and smelling of Brut 64, the Prime Minister's personal aroma, I was — presented to Cabinet! Here was the test — before the leader's personal friends and enemies. . . .

VOICE COACH [*whispering, expectant*] : Ready, Mr Searle? Head down a little, almost as if you're going to gore somebody — that's it — and as you walk on, list to the right slightly — you're on!

[*Sounds of footfalls across a platform.*]

SEARLE [*clearing his throat*] : Who Calls These Troubled Times? That, gentlemen, is the question I wish to speak about tonight, but before I do so, let me confess at once to a feeling of disappointment at the recent decision by the commission, which can only add to inflationary pressures at this point of time. The wage increases handed down by this august body can only further discourage employers

from taking on additional employees — or indeed from even replacing natural wastage in the workforce. ... [*To himself, in a whisper*] Thump the lectern now, thump the lectern. ... [*Aloud*] The learned gentlemen have [*thumping*] *failed to recognize* the obvious link between wages and unemployment and can therefore only [*thumping*] *delay the time* when the economy can be restored, when industry will expand its output, when *everybody* will be gainfully employed, when the divisions amongst us shall be healed, and we shall be [*thumps*] *one people, one party, and one nation.*
[*applause and hear hears.*]
[*Talking to himself*] The applause went to my head, old actor that I am, and I had to be restrained from giving an encore.... Ministers of state approached me incredulous, offering me congratulations, cigars — but the officials, fearful perhaps that too close a contact would ruin the illusion so carefully created, led me away to His Excellency's private apartments, where Johnson, my faithful valet, was waiting, and where, in monogrammed pyjamas, between sheets of silk, and in the arms of the great god Mogadon ... Mogadon, Mogadoon, Mogadown, down, down, I fell asleep.
[*Sounds of knocking.*]
[*Nervous, suddenly awakened*] Who is it? Who's there?
JOHNSON : It's me sir, Johnson. [*sound of door opening.*] Breakfast. Porridge, scrambled eggs and bacon. His Honour's favourites. He'd sit up in bed with his breakfast on one side and his document box on the other ... eyes-only memoranda — cables in from the consulates — latest reports from all over the world — petitions — summaries — selections from the morning papers....
SEARLE : I'd rather like that. I'd like a look at all that, if I could — with my porridge.
JOHNSON : Sorry sir, I'm not supposed to — a boxless breakfast — they were my instructions.
SEARLE : A look, a peep, over my porridge.
JOHNSON [*wavering*] : It's irregular sir. Highly irregular.
SEARLE : The box — come on — be a devil — aha!
JOHNSON : Easy sir — please —
SEARLE [*reading while fending him off*] : Eyes PM Only — "the

situation in the canned fruit industry can only be described as desperate — if words won't move you, perhaps these illustrations will" — hand-lettered on parchment, with tiny illuminations of withered orchards, fruit rotting on the vine. . . . I am moved, gentlemen, but am PM only for a day. . . . Good grief, what's this about America, code-named Armorica? The President is what? Oh come on —

JOHNSON [*struggling*] : I'm sorry sir, I'll have to have that box, thank you very much. Matters of [*grabbing box*] national moment. Have your eggs sir — you'll need the nourishment. This box, it's needed at once — and so are you. I have to dress you in five minutes — might I hope for a little more co-operation — we won't have time for any more horseplay and fooling. Seven forty-five you have to be dressed and ready. Eight fifteen we emplane.

SEARLE : Emplane? Barbarous usage, barbarous. To where, Johnson, to where?

JOHNSON : Melbourne sir, that's the whisper going round the office. Aboard your own personal aircraft — red, white, and blue telephones, bar, bedroom, bathroom, eight-track stereo — the lot.

[*fade out. Fade in sounds of Beethoven, and up. Searle is humming and singing to the music.*]

SEARLE [*to himself*] : I could pick up the blue phone and talk to my sister in London . . . the white phone, and all our jet fighters would go on red alert — all fifteen of 'em — tempting. God, look at that — all Australia spread out below me —

[*discreet knock.*]

ANDERSON : How are we this morning? This is Mr Lampedusa. [*Sounding a little scornful*] Mr Lampedusa is in public relations.

SEARLE : How do you do.

LAMPEDUSA : Superb. Just superb.

ANDERSON : Could we have the two-minute off-the-cuff airport-lounge meet-the-media speech? For Mr Lampedusa. Go.

SEARLE : Ladies and gentlemen — let me say first how much I regret the fact that I can give you only the fewest of moments — my time is short because my day is so long. Let me say second what a pleasure it is to be back in your stately and beautiful city — all those parks — I saw them from the aircraft — such a contrast to the crispbreads of the inland — a garden city, all vigour and life — and while on the subject of vigour and life, I'd like to scotch once and for all the baseless rumours circulated by some of your media brothers that I am, or was, ill, incapacitated, or unable to carry out my duties —

LAMPEDUSA : Wrong, wrong!

ANDERSON : What d'you mean, wrong? Show them up for the gossip-mongers they are.

LAMPEDUSA : One — a resentful media is an uncooperative media, and that's what you'll make 'em with remarks like that. Two — it is unwise to refer even to the *possibility* of the Prime Minister's being ill. Our studies have shown —

PILOT'S VOICE OVER INTERCOM : All safety belts to be fastened please. Safety belts fastened.

ANDERSON : — never mind about your studies. Our whole strategy has been based on showing the flag, on proving he's still in there fighting, aloof, masterful, in command, reassuring the faint-hearts, banging the lectern —

LAMPEDUSA : He's here, isn't he? Fit and well, tangible, palpable — isn't that enough? No need to spell it out — by referring to a rumour, you only acknowledge its strength, give the Gold Crosses heart —

SEARLE : What? The Gold Cross? The old secret society?

ANDERSON : Opposition to your good self, Mr Searle, and to everything you represent, is now crystallizing round the trusty gentlemen of the Golden Cross. We're pleased. We'll let it focus, develop a little, and then — boom!

SEARLE : So — you're setting me up — to bring them out into the open?

LAMPEDUSA : To polarize 'em, Mr Searle, to polarize. We'll be able to see how strong they are.

SEARLE : And if they're too strong, what happens then? I could be assassinated.

ANDERSON : Ten secret servicemen, everywhere you go. Everywhere!

[*sounds of jets in reverse thrust.*]

SEARLE : Whassat? Bombs?

ANDERSON : Calm down! We've landed! Haven't you been on a jet before?

SEARLE : I'm a train traveller. . . . Do I say my little airport piece or don't I?

ANDERSON : You do!

LAMPEDUSA : You don't!

ANDERSON : Do!

LAMPEDUSA : Don't!

SEARLE : Stop it! You're sapping my confidence!

ANDERSON : A Valium, quickly, to make him statesmanlike and aloof! Two milligrams makes him calm, five milligrams dignified, ten makes him a statesman! . . . It's your fault, you got him upset — you PR people are nothing but trouble.

SEARLE [*practising speech to himself*] : Ladies and gentlemen — let me say first how much I regret the fact that I can give you only the fewest of moments — silly phrase, silly silly phrase. [*To himself*] What's that noise in the distance? A band? The cheers of the crowd? When the door opens, stand at the top of the steps, join your hands and raise them high. . . . [*Aloud, suddenly*] I feel fear! Apprehension! Terror!

ANDERSON : They're waiting for you! This is your doing, Lampedusa!

LAMPEDUSA : Nonsense. I'm here to calm the man, give him confidence —

SEARLE : I can't!

ANDERSON : Into that doorway!

[*"Advance Australia Fair" breaks out. Cheers, in three rhythmical waves. Appropriate mumblings — How d'you do — How d'you do — as he meets VIPs.*]

SEARLE [*to himself*] : I was introduced to an assortment of dignitaries, cringers, fawners and petty officials, who seemed even more frightened than I was . . . and then hustled to the VIP lounge and exhibited, like a kind of talking totem, to the media. . . . I was led to the rostrum, introduced, applauded, photographed, televised. Then my mouth opened, and, programmed, I spoke — it was me and yet not me. I spoke and listened at the same time, my words emerging and returning from me simultaneously. [*Making speech, but with wave-like distortions*] I want to say first, ladies and gentlemen, how much I regret the fact that I can

give you only the fewest of moments — my time is short
because my day is so long. Let me say second what a
pleasure it is to be back in your stately and beautiful city —
all those parks — I saw them from the aircraft — a garden
city, all vigour and life. I'd like to scotch once and for all
the baseless rumours . . . .
[*Fade away.*]
[*To himself*] Did I finish the speech? Yes, I finished the
speech, and then they shotgunned me with questions —
hordes of journalists, so sharp, so seagull-eyed, crowding in
upon me for a crust, a crumb that they could peck at —

VOICES [*overlapping, building, getting more frenetic*] : Is it true
sir, you made a clandestine visit to a Sydney kidney
specialist?

— the wages decision, Prime Minister, were you happy with
that?

— what is your policy on Antarctica?

— are you buying Cocos Island?

— has the F-111 replacement been decided upon?

— inflation — your policy has failed, has it not?

— one of your most senior ministers — is it true he's on a
drunk driving charge?

— do you realize it's nearly twelve months since you've
been to Melbourne?

— resources tax? Yes or no?

— nuclear safeguards agreement, what's happening?

— air fares, when do they drop?

— drug trafficking — how are you going to stop it?

— canned fruit industry — your measures are?

SEARLE [*initially trying to answer, but after being cut across by
question after question, roars in desperation*] : NO
COMMENT! [*To himself*] The limousine, quickly!
[*As he hurries to it he's followed by more shouted
questions, perhaps a mix of the above, a wild babble which
gradually recedes.*]
[*To flunkey*] Never mind about the formality, just open it!
[*Car door opening and closing.*]
[*To himself*] Phew! . . . God, what upholstery. Like lolling
on stuffed gloves. . . . A motorcade! All the way to the city!
[*background of siren noises.*] Outriders on great silver

Yamahas in crimson helmets and leggings of blue leather,
green-and-gold pennants snapping from the five-feet
antlers of their handlebars. . . . Mercedes to the front of me,
Rollses behind, and in the middle of this awesome, blaring,
strident, and flashing cavalcade, in a Bentley like an
upholstered battleship, me, Edward Searle, clerk, citizen,
man in the street — standing in a huge bullet-proof bubble
of perspex, arms high, fingers signalling out triumphant V
for Victory signs! . . . Crowd barriers everywhere, but where
are the crowds? A few groups of captive schoolchildren at
intersections, some old ladies pausing with their jeeps on
the way to the shops, and there, on the wall by the
supermarket, a single defiant gold cross. . . .

[*Noise of sirens up, then out.*]

[*Bonging noise, as of single clock-strike.*]

JOHNSON [*announcing*] : Ten fifteen a.m. Courtesy call on State
Governor.

[*ceremonial music, fading into . . .*]

SEARLE [*talking to himself*] : He received me on the lawns
before his impressive Italianate mansion, classified A by
the National Trust. *He* ought to be as well . . . reddest face
I've ever seen . . . I bow to him first — this is his last
territory — the divine right of kings has come to this, this
sad little piece of pompous protocol. He bows in return. Can
you bow sardonically? This little Englander does just that
— his obsequiousness is theatrical and patronizing. As his
head goes down, the strawberry hues purple to loganberry,
and the blood seems to throb visibly through the slick of
white hairstands. Will he explode? No, and he won't talk
either — all vice-regal self-importance, he waits for me to
make the running . . . damned if I will. We stand there
facing but not looking at one another, surrounded by aides
and flunkeys, in total and ludicrous silence. Who'll speak?
Who'll break first? Throne or Commons? Aha — he
weakens, he points to the sky, inclines his head, and utters!
[*Sound of asinine mumblings.*] I agree with him — the
weather is indeed sunny.

[*Bonging noise.*]

JOHNSON [*announcing*] : Eleven   a.m.   —   Outer-suburban
community centre to be declared open.

SEARLE [*to himself*] : What bleakness! Wind whistling across the factories, the flatlands ... new houses on muddy roads leading to nowhere ... [*roar of low plane.*] Only thing they're handy to out here's the airport ... population largely Slavonic ... secret service form a Vee phalanx as I walk through them to inspect gymnasium, library, pool ... swarthy fellows — five o'clock shadows, blunt features, sharp suits ... initially uncertain, deferential ... but when I cut the ribbon and declare the dreary place open [*Few words of Yugoslavian.*] in their own language, the result is amazing, they go mad — [*Babblings, shoutings.*] — the air's filled with shouts, laughs, and the quick karate-chops of their gesticulations. One man becomes so carried away he tries a direct frontal approach and gets to within a couple of feet of me, arms wide. Embrace or attack? My men drag him away, taking no chances.
[*Bonging noise.*]

JOHNSON [*announcing*] : Twelve noon. [*Brief Jewish sacred music.*] Witness dedication of synagogue.
[*Bonging noise.*]
One o'clock. [*Brief Arab music.*] Lay foundation stone of mosque.
[*Bonging noise.*]
One thirty. Working lunch.
[*Hum of confidential converse, discreet clacking of cutlery, crockery, pop of cork.*]

SEARLE [*to himself*] : I'm congratulated, but not as effusively as I'd expected. My goatee had become slightly askew, and I was politely taken to task for not noticing it. No good being ninety-five per cent PM, one of them added, in a tone I didn't care for. ... Strange fellows — just when you're getting a feeling for the part, they sap your confidence.
[*Bonging noise.*]

JOHNSON [*announcing*] : Three o'clock. New trade offices to be opened in St Kilda Road.

SEARLE [*to himself*] : Compliment First Assistant Secretary on design — though actually found it detestable. Concrete bunker on the outside, vast inhuman spaces on the inside— clerks by the hundred cowering behind potted palms — perhaps even they, like me, are plastic. ... Amazing —

whenever someone important descends upon the lowly, they always expect one thing — a speech. Doesn't matter how vacuous or stupid — it's the form of the thing that's expected . . . instead of talking to people you make speeches.
. . .
[*Clears throat. Discreet applause. Instead of making a connected speech, he recites phrases, first with a weighty pause between each, later one after the other rapidly, building up to an impressive peroration.*]
World trade talks . . . multilateral negotiations . . . morass of protectionism . . . access to European Economic Community . . . Australian primary products . . . lift living standards . . . underdeveloped nations . . . across the board . . . trade-off with Japan . . . co-prosperity sphere . . . they buy our beef, we buy their cars . . . international economic stability . . . Prices Justification Tribunal . . . burden of inflation . . . farmers driven off their land . . . lynchpin of our strategy . . . stakes involved . . . thrust of our policy!
[*Discreet applause.*]
[*Bonging noise.*]

JOHNSON [*announcing*] : Four o'clock. Meet-the-people stroll through shopping centre.

SEARLE [*to himself*] : I'm assured the applause is spontaneous, but it seems to be rehearsed . . . it stops and starts at regular intervals, as if conducted by a secret cheerleader —
[*appropriate background sounds.*]
— with a strange, almost ethereal hissing in the intervals, as though coming from the sky.
[*Hissing sounds, subtle.*]
Here, in this middle-class heartland, I sense hostility without actually seeing it . . . my men look around for the source of the secret sibilations, but are unable to track them down . . .
Angry at their failure, they take out their frustrations on a lone demonstrator, a ragged eccentric with a placard on which is written Flesh Meat Equals Protein Equals Lust. Quite mad and quite harmless, but he has his sign broken over his head. While my guardians are thus busily engaged, I alone notice, in the distance, on the first floor of the

arcade, a man in a gift shop wave a golden dagger. Is he examining it with the intention of purchasing, or is it a gesture of defiance? I let it pass.

[*Bonging noise.*]

JOHNSON [*announcing*] : A quarter to five. Gymnastic display by schoolchildren at Cricket Ground.

SEARLE [*to himself, periodically swamped by cheers*] : Children by the thousand, fidgeting and restive because they've been kept waiting for over an hour. They go through their routines mechanically [*Sounds of drilling whistles.*] — ragged coloured squares, sluggish turning circles, the touching of ten thousand toes . . . the highlight of the afternoon a rendering of my likeness in flashcards. After complicated and indescribably tedious manoeuvres, they regroup and [*Whistle*] all the cards suddenly flash up at me in unison — but the ear contingent has moved too near the cheekbone group, so that the organ seems to hang from the bone as if I've been slashed. Officials beside themselves with embarrassment. Despite my assurances to the contrary, they know I am shocked, see me go pale. As I leave, schoolmasters race onto oval to apprehend culprits.

[*Bonging noise.*]

SEARLE [*to himself*] : On the stroke of seven, Johnson, my faithful valet, trusses me in white tie and tails for the Lord Mayor's Annual Dinner at the Melbourne Town Hall. . . .

JOHNSON : Easy, sir, easy —

SEARLE : This is ridiculous . . . feels like chain-mail . . . I'm getting damned sick of this — this charade, posturing and parading . . .

JOHNSON : Work *with* your apparel sir, not against it. Otherwise you'll waddle, sir, all over the place like a penguin. . . . Don't fight your garments, give in to 'em — walk a bit slower, a bit of dignity . . . that's better . . . lovely . . . poetry in motion. The secret's in the leisurely gait, sir.

SEARLE : It's my neck. I can move my legs, and manage my arms — but the collar's too tight — ridiculous . . . plastic prime minister . . . celluloid supremo.

JOHNSON : If we undo the button the tie mightn't sit straight —

SEARLE : I can't breathe — I can't swallow — how can I get through four courses if I can't swallow —

JOHNSON : — you're not used to it sir, that's the problem.

SEARLE : — I *can't* get used to not breathing — nor to being PM. I'm sick and tired of the whole business.

JOHNSON : Come on sir, cheer up — you're rounding the home turn now and into the straight. This dinner's your farewell appearance. Positively. After that, nothing ... finito.

SEARLE [*to himself*] : Seven thirty ... break away from official party as instructed for unscheduled chat with old lady in the crowd around Town Hall steps ...

OLD LADY : — Oh, Your Excellency!

SEARLE : — all the very best to you, my dear. Trust you haven't been waiting long.

OLD LADY : — Your Excellency! I'm speechless! You do look well! All these rumours about your health!

SEARLE : — ignore them. Here I am, in the flesh. Ciao.

OLD LADY [*to the crowd*] : He spoke to me! He spoke to me!

SEARLE [*to himself*] : Up the steps, starched, stiff and studded ... at the top welcomed by His Worship the Mayor, in a strange floppy black hat, as if he's just got his doctorate ... around his neck, an enormous chain, which clinks and rattles as he bows ... heraldic emblems for every Melbourne municipality — is that a gold cross I see worked into the city's coat of arms — or merely a shield, cruciform and gilded? He bows, he scrapes, his aldermanic apparatus seems to silver the ground. ...

MAYOR : — Your Excellency! What an honour for the city! The queen city of the south! The garden city! Racing, football, cultural and ecclesiastical city! [*More confidentially*] Freeways, overpasses, undergrounds — keep us in mind, excellence, when the grants are apportioned. ... [*aloud*] this way, this way — see what spectacles and wonders we have prepared for you. ... [*more confidentially again*] Keep us in mind, I beseech you, when the allocations are being decided ... *le voila*!

SEARLE [*to himself*] : What a sight! The entire auditorium re-decorated to resemble a large bushland clearing ... ferns, trees and native plants rear up all around us — and about an actual waterfall a host of indigenous creatures are gathered — borrowed, my host tells me, from the museum:

kangaroo and koala, lyrebird and lorrikeet, cockatoo and cassowary, possum and platypus. ... As we enter, all the guests stand, and birdsongs break out, as if we had plunged into the wilds!

[*Appropriate noises.*]

We proceed with ceremony up the aisle, and as we walk up the steps to the table of honour, sweet music from hidden strings. [*Over a waltz*] Are they there, behind the eucalypts? Or is it in the fern gully I see the shimmer of bows? *Son et lumiere*, look at this — above the official table, a magnificent centrepiece — a diorama depicting Melbourne's founding: the Aborigines happy with their mirrors and beads, and John Batman holding the title for the land! This is indeed the place for a village.

[*Music up, over and down.*]

We sit, and so too does the entire distinguished assemblage, their medals winking silver and gold under the chandeliers — returned soldiers almost all, by the look of them ... and what food — Turtle Soup King Island, Venison Rouge Orbost, Compote des Fruits Shepparton, rare Mildura Shirazes, ripe Rutherglen Ports ... the plate is gold, the tablecloths crimson, the company convivial, the atmosphere expectant.

[*Sounds of discreetly convivial wining and dining.*]

But wait, here's something strange ... the hubbub, at first comparatively hearty, instead of increasing as one would expect when fine wine is flowing, seems — do I imagine it — to *recede* with each course — no, I *don't* imagine it — so that by dessert there's almost total silence ... yes! Only His Tedious Worship the Mayor and myself seem to be struggling on with conversation, our voices audible all over the hall. ...

MAYOR [*slightly strained*] : More wine, Excellence?

SEARLE [*also strained*] : No thank you very much.

MAYOR : An excellent vintage. Tantalizing nose, and fine fruity finish.

SEARLE : Very fruity finish. Like the last movement of Beethoven's Ninth — crescendo!

MAYOR : I prefer Gilbert and Sullivan myself. Something with a tune you can hum.

SEARLE [*to himself*] : Everyone can hear us . . . all over the hall
— listening . . . I become nervous, my hand trembles round
the goblet's crystal stem. Is it me they're staring at, or is it
John Batman and the Aborigines behind? My beard? My
silver curls? What are they *waiting* for? Is it my speech? My
speech! At once! Without introductions! Before the tension
becomes unendurable! [*Getting to his feet and addressing
them suddenly*] Who Calls These Troubled Times? That,
gentlemen, is the question I wish to speak about tonight,
but before I do so, let me confess at once to a feeling of disappointment at the recent decision by the Commission,
which can only add to inflationary pressures at this point of
time.
[*Bang of gong, not too loud.*]
[*Faltering*] Inflationary pressures . . . point of time. . . .
[*Regaining poise*] The wage increases handed down by
this august body can only further discourage employers
from taking on additional employees. . . . [*To himself*]
Why do the men at that table stand? . . . march to the
steps? . . . ascend? [*Regaining poise*] — or indeed from
even *replacing* natural wastage from the workforce. The
learned gentlemen have *failed to recognize* the link between
wage increases and unemployment, and can therefore only
delay the time when the economy can be — [*weakening*]
restored. . . . [*To himself*] What are they doing up here on
the platform with that cutlery? Those knives of gold? Why
do my men move back and not forward? Gold knife — Gold
Cross! The secret society! Aah! [*Still to himself, but
faster*] I twist in my chair at the last minute — and dart for
the bush — [*puffing*] stumbling and jumping over
bracken, leaping the waterfall, racing for the cover of the
trees! [*Gunshot*] My god! Inches away a wallaby explodes
in a shower of stuffing! Faster, faster! I run, run, till behind
a tall fern I see a door! [*sound of door being wrenched
open.*] Aha! Through dim, deserted offices I speed, to dark
stairs, and down — to the street, where, god save me, there's
a cab! . . . All this happened but a short time ago. Lonely,
afraid, I write this message, as agents and officials, like
beaters, work their way steadily through the city.
[*Hoarsely*] Help me!

Other Plays Published by University of Queensland Press